WHAT NEXT

The Art of Bouncing Back

Cdr Bimal Raj (retd)

Chennai • Bangalore

CLEVER FOX PUBLISHING
Chennai, India

Published by CLEVER FOX PUBLISHING 2023
Copyright © Cdr Bimal Raj 2023

All Rights Reserved.
ISBN: 978-93-56485-18-1

This book has been published with all reasonable efforts taken to make the material error-free after the consent of the author. No part of this book shall be used, reproduced in any manner whatsoever without written permission from the author, except in the case of brief quotations embodied in critical articles and reviews.

The Author of this book is solely responsible and liable for its content including but not limited to the views, representations, descriptions, statements, information, opinions and references ["Content"]. The Content of this book shall not constitute or be construed or deemed to reflect the opinion or expression of the Publisher or Editor. Neither the Publisher nor Editor endorse or approve the Content of this book or guarantee the reliability, accuracy or completeness of the Content published herein and do not make any representations or warranties of any kind, express or implied, including but not limited to the implied warranties of merchantability, fitness for a particular purpose. The Publisher and Editor shall not be liable whatsoever for any errors, omissions, whether such errors or omissions result from negligence, accident, or any other cause or claims for loss or damages of any kind, including without limitation, indirect or consequential loss or damage arising out of use, inability to use, or about the reliability, accuracy or sufficiency of the information contained in this book.

Cover Design by Vivekananda Roy Ghatak

Dedication

*Pallavi, Giaa, my fur babies, both sets of parents and sisters…
and Raju, of course!*

CONTENTS

Foreword..*v*
Acknowledgements ....*vii*
Prologue..*xiv*

1. Roots..1
2. The Shift 12
3. A Spiritual Escapade 26
4. The Truth Is…Subjective?..33
5. The Lowest Forms of Marine Life 45
6. The Death Bridge and the Demons 61
7. Find Your Feet (Figuratively, Of Course!) 86
8. Love Is A Smoke..98
9. Amor Fati 120
10. Uncharted Waters..133
11. Better to Light the Candle 159
12. Opportunities Find You!...182
13. The Predicaments in a Pandemic 196
14. The What Next Mindset 204
15. The What Next Method 221
16. The Action Plan..235

What Next…After What Next!..*252*
Epilogue...*253*

FOREWORD

This is a book about grit, perseverance, and the power of the human spirit. The first time I met Bimal was in a training room, and little did I know about his past. But the more I interacted with him, the more I got to know about his large-heartedness and his core desire to help people succeed.

Bimal has always been approachable and genuine, and his training with some of the best mentors in the world has resulted in a global understanding of human problems. I have seen firsthand how his empathy and ability to connect with people using his experiences and learnings has brought a turn-around in their lives.

What Next is a book about the willingness to take chances in the face of immense failures. Incredible bad luck, bad timing, and bad judgment have all been thorns in Bimal's life, thorns he has effectively plucked out and learnt to continue walking, dreaming, and growing. He is a living example of how to bounce back when life throws lemons at you. His book showcases raw emotions in situations any of us can fall prey to, and he offers suggestions and thoughts on how to overcome them based on his own experience.

As I read through the pages of this incredible book, tears welled up in my eyes as I realized the depth of Bimal's wisdom and the profound impact it would have on my life. Every chapter spoke directly to my heart, touching on the raw emotions and experiences that make us human. Bimal has poured his soul onto these pages, bringing together his life's journey with timeless principles to help us all reach our full potential.

As a fellow student of Blair Singer, I felt an instant connection with him and his message. Bimal has captured the very essence of what it means to be a leader of your own life, and his words have moved me in ways I never thought possible. I cannot recommend this book enough, and I urge anyone who wants to make a positive change in their life to read it and be inspired.

Often, we come across impossible situations, and at times like this, we can only see the dark. We forget that light is just around the corner. This book is about not giving up, not letting the world decide when you are done. It's about being a warrior who will not stop until they find the light. This book is for you, me, and anyone who wishes to know that their struggles are valid, that they are not alone, and that they will find glory if they only continue to ask the question - What Next?

Siddharth Rajsekar
Founder - Internet Lifestyle Hub
India's Leading Digital Coach

ACKNOWLEDGEMENTS

A FRIEND, A BROTHER, AND A GUARDIAN ANGEL

I have been really blessed in my life because of my parents, sisters, in-laws and a whole bunch of friends but this individual stands head and shoulders above all my friends and well-wishers—Srinivas Raju Mantena (Raju for me), someone to whom I owe most of what I have achieved in my life, especially after Navy. I can attribute most of my amazing success and experiences in life to his unconditional and unhindered support throughout. I can count on him in the worst situations in my life. He has seen me and supported me at my worst, whether it was my physical health, financial, emotional or any other challenge in my life. He has been a constant and I can say that my life today is stress-free largely due to his presence in my life. He may not be the most expressive person I have come across, but he is like a rock. Not just me, but there are many others whom he has helped all through, knowing well that there is nothing much that I or the others can do to reciprocate. It is just who he is. An amazing and unconditional human being. He reminds me of the punching bag. I have lost count of the number of challenges he's faced in life, but after every single punch, he comes right back to the centre, ready to keep going. I am so inspired by him that I have always wanted to start a trust in his name to help those with big dreams but lack the resources to achieve them. It is on my bucket list. Maybe one day…

MY FAMILY

Pallavi has been my biggest strength from the time she came into my life. Her belief, her support and her love and dedication are unconditional. She has encouraged me in my every endeavour, believed in me, and contributed immensely to whatever I did. If she couldn't contribute physically, she became the biggest supporter. She looks like a trophy wife (yeah, she does) but in reality, she is a simple, kind, expressive and fun-loving person with no demands except that I love her and spend time with her. I am genuinely and deeply thankful to her for enduring me and loving me all these years. Many times, I look at her and think of how lucky I am to have her as my life partner in my life.

The light of my life, Giaa-Marie... She completes me. I started studying parenting a couple of decades back because I wanted to have a great relationship with my child, and I am so glad that I did. We connect very deeply and not just as a father and daughter but also as two individuals who can talk about things in life, what we are going through and even our aspirations. Pal and I have never tried to "protect" her from the challenges that we have had in our lives. We always make it a point to have engaging conversations with her as well, like the kind of books she reads. Some of the conversations that we have are just something to treasure. She is still a child and loves to have fun and I love to irritate her with my 'dad jokes'. Without her, our lives would have been incomplete.

My *Achan* and *Amma* and my two sisters, Minichechi and Jochechi who loves me as their son and encouraged me (they still do) in everything I do in my life. I learned the motto 'Family comes first' by being in this family. I am lucky and privileged to be born into this family. My sisters took care of me and looked out for me all through my life and they still do. I am very lucky and blessed to have these two wonderful and loving "mothers" in my life (psst… don't tell them).

My in-laws, Papa and Mamma, who have been (and still are) a huge support all through our married lives. They have been there as the strongest support in our downs and cheered us on as we progressed. They both have played hockey for India; Papa has been the head coach for the Indian hockey women's team for over 20 years and has travelled the world as an International Umpire. I still feel at times that he got the wrong son-in-law because I have no interest in playing or even watching hockey. They are one of the most selfless, accommodating, and caring parents I have ever come across. I stopped being their son-in-law and became their son long ago. I have spent a lot of time with both and I have tremendous love and respect for them. Even now, when we have a need, the first call goes to them.

MY SCULPTORS

Blair Singer – The one person I consider to be my Mentor. Someone I aspire to be like in values, commitment and skills. He taught me that if I want to HAVE something, I must BE that person who deserves it. I am yet to see someone who is so captivating. He taught me about being the most effective and authentic trainer and teacher and he did it by just being who is. I learned everything about being a world-class trainer from him more than anyone else. I am proud to be part of his chosen tribe through BSTA (Blair Singer Training Academy)

Mac Attram was my first lead trainer at MMI (Millionaire Mind Intensive). Incidentally, he was also the lead trainer when I attended MMI (less than two years before I went on stage with him) where the desire to be on that stage germinated. It was a dream come true moment when I got to share the stage with him. He is one of the humblest of human beings He is a man of few words and as the lead trainer, he wants you to succeed and grow and he gives a multitude of opportunities to his trainers and constantly encourages them to shine on stage. It's magical to see him in action. He is never the same in two different cities. He transforms according to what the participants need on a daily basis.

Robert Raymond Riopel, my other lead trainer for MMI. He is the only person who teaches Enlightened Warrior Power (how!) and with him, there is not a single dull moment. He is very clear about what he expects from his trainers and guides in every step of the way. I was able to spend some good personal time with him and his lovely wife Roxanne during an MMI in Vietnam. We have an excellent connection at a personal level and he has given me the rare privilege where I can get on calls with him any time I need help/support.

Thaddeus Lawrence was the Assistant Trainer that I worked with the most. He is an exceptional trainer and a brother to me. I was lucky to have spent a lot of time with him as my AT, and we were also in the same team when we did the Ultimate Personal Development Program of Blair at Arizona, where we connected at a different level as well.

It has been my privilege to work with these amazing trainers at MMI.

Siddharth Rajsekar, Sidz for us is one of those rare individuals that we don't get to see these days. I have seen him from his initial struggling days to now when he is super successful, and he has not changed one tiny bit. Still the humblest, and most endearing person who is always ready to go the extra mile to help. He is a true inspiration to us. Sidz and Vanitha have been our greatest encouragers, and supporters all through our journey as a trainer-coach. The world would be such a beautiful place to live if there were more and more people like them.

Surendran Jayasekar or Suren is another person who saw me and chose me. He encouraged me in every step of the way. He has always looked out for Pal and me. He followed up with us regularly during the pandemic to see how we were doing. He is family to us. Someone who genuinely wants to see us succeed and do big things in life. He owns one of the largest training companies in the country, but he is someone who we can relate to and talk to as a friend and brother. That is a rare quality.

Rajiv Talreja and Bhakti who have constantly encouraged me and supported me in my training journey. Even though an extremely busy person, they found time to sit with me and help me with my parenting program. When I was struggling to give shape to all the knowledge that I had gained, it was Rajiv who asked me *'Bimal, how can you develop a scientific approach to parenting? Something that would work every time in every situation?'* Those were the seeds that helped me structure my program in such a way that it worked every time in every situation.

Betska K-Burr and John K-Burr—my coaching Gurus, who are amazing human beings and kind-hearted souls who helped me become a world-class Mind Kinetics coach. I have been able to touch and transform so many lives through the methodologies that they taught through Coaching and Leadership International, Canada.

MY BUDDIES

I have written in detail about them They helped me understand true friendship, about being there for each other, and not counting the closeness based on the number of calls made each year. The bond we have is made of titanium.

My BSTA buddies **Sudhir Khot and Kalyan Hatti** who are two people I can count on anytime. We have grown close like brothers, and I will always consider them as two of my closest buddies.

I want to thank all my coursemates from **NEC 8**. The bond we share can't be expressed in words. We just know that we are always there for each other.

A special thank you to **Meghana Dixit** or Megs, as we fondly call her. She has always volunteered to help both of us through our struggles and challenges. I love her for the way she always looks out for Pal, for being her soul sister and for being someone we can always count on.

THE BOOK THIEVES — THE TRIO!

A best friend is someone who is supposed to annoy you, irritate you, laugh their hearts out when you're in trouble and then go all out to get you out of it. It's someone who will tell you what an ass you are on your face but project you as God's gift to mankind to the rest of the world. A partner in crime when it comes to making fun of others or cracking lame jokes that no one else finds funny. It's someone you can count on or call for help at 3 am (if you manage to wake them up) and know for sure that they would turn up. You have been all that and so much more, **Uma Seshadri Iyer**. I still have no clue how you not only believed that there was a writer in me, but you managed to harass and nag this book out of me. Life is fun when there are cracked friends like you around (shoulder dance). Stop laughing!

My editor **Suma Nagaraj**, who transformed this book and raised its level many notches with her insistence on my rewriting certain parts, adding more information, and removing some redundant ones (giving a deaf ear to my groans and ignoring pained looks). She has been on the task from day one, thank you for not letting me off the hook and making me finish what I started. If any of you reading this needs an editor, trust me, look no further!

I am indebted to **Vivekananda Roy Ghatak** (Viv to us), who volunteered to design the cover of the book, just to show his support. He is an animation film director and the co-founder of an animation company Rocket Science Animation. He has won multiple awards like Cannes World Film Festival 2023, Animators Guild India 2023 and many more but that never stopped him from taking his precious time out to design the cover for me. We discussed different versions and aspects of how the cover should be (actually, it was Viv and Uma discussing and me giving moral support by providing samosa and hot chai from our Bharat Chaat).

Dear reader,

This book is the story of my life, with all its ups and downs. There are places where I have changed names of some people to protect their identity. This in no way alters the storyline.

Happy reading.

PROLOGUE

The pain was excruciating. I realised that my the years of military training were not of much help. I just didn't want to get up in the morning and face the day. The pain wasn't just physical, it was also mental and emotional. At times, I felt I was in an endless abyss. At other times, I could see the walls of my room that had turned grey and black, trying to close in on me. I was scared to go out. My head was always down, and the constant churn in my heart and stomach refused to stop. I dreamt and fantasised about different scenarios where the event that brought me to this stage didn't happen. I tried convincing myself that one day when I woke up, everything would be normal. I felt betrayed by others, I felt that I had let down my parents, and my future looked uncertain and scary.

I had never been exposed to a situation where I had to resolve my challenges on my own, like in this situation. I had my parents, teachers and childhood friends who always helped me and gave me advice on what my next course of action should be. But none of them were there with me now. My room felt cold and looked colourless. The people around me looked at me with sympathy and gave me 'space', as they put it. I was groping in the dark, in despair, trying to find, and hoping for a miracle.

As days turned into weeks, I had a painful realization:

No one was coming to save me.

No one was going to show me how to get out of the pit that I was in.

No one was there to give me a different perspective and reduce the pain that I was carrying around.

I realised for the first time in my life that if I had to move forward, I had to depend on the one person I had never really counted on before—**ME!**

I had to stand up and face my demons myself. I had to figure out a way to reduce my pain and misery, and more than anything, I had to find out from myself—What Next?

CHAPTER 1

ROOTS

I come from Trivandrum, the capital of the Indian state of Kerala or Thiruvananthapuram, as it is officially called now. Quite a tongue twister for the hordes of foreign tourists who flock every year to this beautiful city which used to have one of the best beaches in the world – Kovalam beach (yeah, really!).

The thing about Trivandrum (as it will be mentioned henceforth purely for the selfish reason of being able to type fast) is that nothing ever really changes there. I left the city in 1991, and in the three decades that I've been away, I can count the changes that have happened there on my fingers (well, almost). I guess that is one of the things I love about the city. It holds a lot of things that are very close to my heart. My parents (of course), one of my dear sisters (let me state here for my health and wellbeing purposes that the other one is also equally dear to me), my closest and oldest friends, the roads, Kanakakunnu Palace, the museum, the zoo, the Secretariat, Indian Coffee House at Shankumugham beach, my schools and my colleges, and so many other things. No wonder I go into a different mood every time I land in Trivandrum. I think my subconscious goes into 'I-am-home' mode.

Trivandrum is not just places and people. It is also the place which taught me about unconditional love, the meaning of friendships, the joy of a crush, as well as the pain of heartbreak. I feel even the wind and the rain speak to me in a language that only I understand.

Among the reasons mentioned above, the two major reasons that evoke nostalgia, love and fondness in my heart are my *Amma*[1] and *Achan*[2]. How can anything about my life be complete without letting you know more about them? Our parents are our roots, our foundation, and the kind of relationship that we have with them has a major impact on our adult lives. Let me introduce them one after the other.

My *Amma*. For me, she is the epitome of unconditional love and patience. She is one of the most patient and calm people I have known in my life. I am yet to hear her shout or scream in a loud voice (but then she is just about 85 years, you see). That doesn't mean that she is not strict or firm. I learned that I can be soft and yet firm like metal, unwavering. I can be simple and plain but still, be steady as a rock for others in my life. I learned that confidence is not necessarily the loud voice that booms from the mountaintop. A whisper spoken from the heart is equally powerful. I remember her in my oldest memories, whether it was her making my favourite snacks for me or putting a wet cloth on my forehead when I had a high fever. It is said that I was born after many years after my second sister, Mini*chechi*[3], and was the result of many prayers and *mannat*[4]. By the time I was born, my sisters had grown out of their 'cute-baby' phase, and it was easy for me to take over

---

[1] Malayalam word for mother
[2] Malayalam word for father
[3] Chechi means elder sister in Malayalam. Doesn't have to be blood relation. Any lady elder may be called Chechi to show respect
[4] Hindi word meaning a wish that one desires to come to fruition

all the hearts around me. I was called *mon* (still I am) which means son in Malayalam. Even my sisters called me *mon* because I was one for them as well. Being much younger and being the only son in a traditional *Malayali*[5] family does have its advantages. I was pampered a lot, especially by *Amma*. Even if I instigated my sisters or got into a physical fight with them as a child, I don't remember facing the flak from her. After all, in her eyes, I was someone who could do no wrong. This phenomenon of me chasing my sisters around continued until one day, while I was chasing them, they suddenly stopped in their tracks and asked themselves, 'Why are *we* running? We are two and much bigger than him.' Well, the chase continued but now in the opposite direction.

We were the classic middle-class family, where parents worked round the clock to make the ends meet. *Amma* was a schoolteacher, and she took educating her children very seriously. She would get up early in the morning (like all middle-class moms), cook for everyone (both breakfast as well as lunch), serve breakfast while making sure that all the kids got up and got ready for school, make lunch boxes for everyone including herself and send all her kids to catch their school transport on time. Today, I have one daughter and ten times more gadgets and equipment to make life easier and when I think of Amma, I think she purposely hid her cape not to scare us. She was a working mom, who had three kids studying at the same time. We could not afford maids initially, we didn't have washing machines, food processors, grinders, juicers, vegetable cutting machines, microwave or even a fridge for a long time. Still, we had the best dishes made at home, washed and ironed clothes, clean plates, and hot food in every meal. Not just normal food. Since we could not afford to go to restaurants or order in like we do today, she made even the sweets and all the assorted snacks that we

---
[5]A person born in Kerala, whose mother tongue is Malayalam

would get in a bakery which were naturally yummier. There was no respite for her ever, I think. Because as kids, we were demanding, and I don't remember any of us helping her out majorly in the kitchen. I have never heard her complain about how bad her life was or give a lecture about what all she was doing for us or how ungrateful we were towards her (which a lot of kids get to hear from parents).

Being a traditional *mallu*[6] family, we were not expressive at all when it came to showing affection. The best way *Amma* expressed her love was through her cooking (she still operates the same way). She has been and still is the foundation for our family, the biggest support for my father, holding fort even when he had to travel or even get posted outside our home city because of his work. Even though she didn't want me to go away, she didn't complain or try to emotionally manipulate me into changing my decision when I got selected for Indian Navy. Instead of curbing my dreams, she let me fly.

My *Achan*. If my patience, calmness, and unconditional love come from *Amma*, my practicality, logical reasoning, attitude to go out of the way to help others where I can and a bit of my sense of humour comes from *Achan*. He is one of the most practical people I have come across. He does not allow his emotions to cloud his judgement (well, most times). I learned from him that people and relationships are more important than material things, it is ok for the house to be a little unkempt as long as the people living in it are happy and loving each other. Despite being in a state government job, he was a dreamer. He constantly strived to give a better life to his family. He started his career as a bus conductor in Kerala State Road Transport Corporation, but he was on the lookout for additional sources of income and took up real estate brokering deals

---

[6]Slang for Malayali

when he was not on duty. I have seen him take up night duty for many months so that he could do the real estate deals during the day. I don't know when he got time to sleep during this time. When we were kids, he bought cows to make sure that we had the best and purest milk instead of having to buy it from outside. I remember a time when we had two cows. He used to put them out to graze during the day. In the evening getting them back to the cow shed was a momentous event. At times, one of them would just decide to take off and run back to the shed and I would see her coming at full speed like a locomotive, dragging hapless *Achan* on the other end of the rope, desperately trying to slow her down. I used to stand on one side of a narrow passage and watch this fun event at every chance I got.

Once, while she was charging back in the evening through the narrow passage and I while trying to reach my position, slipped and fell right on the path of the oncoming locomotive called Meenakshi (yes, that was the name of our favourite cow). *Achan* saw this and was visibly scared because Meenakshi was huge and there was no way he could even slow her down. She came charging but when she came near me, she took a leap and jumped over me into a ditch and also into *Achan*'s heart because that jump was difficult for her, but she ensured that she did not harm me at all.

I remember that we had a scooter and later an Ambassador car (all second-hand), but we had these at different times of our growing-up years. The money for these luxuries was made through his real estate deals. He didn't do extremely well because both *Amma* and *Achan* had very high integrity and it does not always serve well if you want to be in a business *and* make money. One of his hallmarks was and still is his amazing sense of humour. Even now, we would knowingly instigate *Achan* to say something about *Amma*'s family when we would be sitting around in the evening and then the fun begins. Both would explain about each other's family in such a way that we would be in splits all the time (*Amma* is no less). There are such hilarious and endearing stories from both of their growing-up years. These conversations are quite unforgettable.

Another aspect that I have imbibed from him is his willingness to help others. It seems there was a time when we were on a single salary during *Amma*'s teacher's training days, and he had to support his brother's family as well. He did not bat an eyelid before taking up that responsibility. His primary aim for all of us—his kids—is that we should have a great relationship with each other, should talk to each other regularly and should be happy and healthy in our individual families. Even now when I call home, conversation with him is always around these few points and it lasts for max three minutes after which he promptly gives the phone back to *Amma* to continue the conversation.

During my orientation course in the Navy, as an icebreaker, all of us were asked who our hero/idol was. Most people gave names of Mahatma Gandhi, Martin Luther King and the like. They are all amazing world leaders who changed the way the world operated. Still, when it came to me, I did not have any hesitation in sharing that for me, my heroes were and will always be my dearest *Amma* and *Achan*.

I have always been very close to my two sisters (Jo*chechi* and Mini*chechi*). Since I was born many years after them, I was not just their kid brother. They naturally took a motherly role towards raising me (me being a very cute baby must have surely helped). They have always loved me and taken care of me like a son (still do) all my life. When they got married and had children of their own, it was a difficult process for them to put their child as the primary one because I had been the primary one for them for too many years of their lives. They keep reminding me about this even now (which gives me the chance to remind them of how old they must be if they consider someone close to 50 years as their child). The pure joy of irritating siblings is priceless – even now.

They took to their roles earnestly. I think they still do at some level. To date, we have a very loving, caring, and deep bond between the three of us. For me, that is priceless.

Another important part of my growing up years were my childhood friends. We were from different schools. So I met most of them at the tuition centre. One of my closest friends to date is Syed. We met at Kiski's (Will tell you about Kiski soon) 9th grade tuition since he was in a different school. We were cordial at first and we grew closer by the day. Soon, most of my weekends and spare time was with him, either at his home or roaming somewhere together. When he went abroad, he made sure that his home visit was always through Mumbai so that we could spend some time together. All of us, friends used to crash at his place during every Eid and Ramadan and eat the delicious mutton biriyani his mom made. We ate till we couldn't move. One of my fondest memories is when, even after not being in touch for months, he drunk-dialled me, just to connect.

Then comes Sivakumar or *Happy*, as we all know him. He got the name because he mostly used to wear the T-Shirt with 'Happy' written on it. It was a very common T-Shirt while we were growing up. When all of us finished our 12th and were trying for engineering, medical, etc, he was the only one bold enough to take up entrepreneurship. I still remember him starting with a small hardware store and today he has a full-fledged IT services company with a staff of over 150 and serving clients all over the world.

I knew Anant or *Pattan* from a very young age as we were together in the school before Christ Nagar, where I did my middle and high schooling. The incident that I remember about us most is when we were together in 3rd-grade dramatics, and we had to go to the venue for our performance. We had carried our lunch from home, and I was sitting next to Pattan, having my lunch. I guess I did not understand what a pure vegetarian meant, and I took pity looking at his lunch box which had plain curd rice. In all my earnestness and love for my friend, I insisted that he has my sardine fish fry along with his bland curd rice. When he politely refused, I made sure that he had a decent lunch by forcefully placing a big sardine right on top of his curd rice. I was neither happy with his reaction (because he was visibly upset), nor with my teacher's long lecture (No marks for intention?).

There are two Krishnakumars. One is called I.S because those are his initials. He is the one person I know, who can't put on weight no matter what he eats. Today, he is with the Salem Steel Plant and is a genius when it comes to technical knowledge. If he comes to know that any of us is in town, he tries to come down at least for a day or two just to catch up. He was also my saviour in college when it came to my second language, French, which I had chosen just because I thought it was very fashionable. I reached a point, that too just weeks before my exams where I could not understand anything I read in French. He promptly invited me home and spent days teaching and helping me understand (while his mom fed me sumptuous meals) and I passed the subject with flying colours.

The second Krishnakumar is *Kikkan*. I met him in college. I saw this tall and thin guy sitting in one corner all alone. I went and spoke with him and learned that he had shifted from a city called Bhilai, which was in the erstwhile state of Madhya Pradesh (now Chhattisgarh). He didn't have many friends around and we connected immediately, and we have been together since. Since we were in the same college and class, we did many group studies, spent time together at college, and discussed state politics, weather, movies, sports and most importantly, the girls in our class. He is also the one person who gave me wholehearted support at a point when I needed it, which is a story for another chapter.

Jayshanker or *Chankaran*, as we call him, was way ahead of all of us lesser mortals when it came to studies and intelligence. He used to talk quantum physics while we tried to figure out how to pass 10th-grade exams. He was clear that he did not want to get into a professional course and went on to do his higher studies abroad and excelled in it. Like most people who excel abroad, he settled down in the US.

I also found two gems when I started playing tennis at the prestigious Trivandrum Tennis Club (TTC). They caused some people to doubt their eyesight (made them think they had double vision) because Deepak (Varkey G George) and Dilip (Abraham G George) were identical twins. There were very few people who could make out who was who and proudly, I was one of them. Even my dad used to say, 'One of them, Deepak-Dilip, came looking for you.' They were quite well off and stayed in a massive house next to the tennis club. We used to openly lust at their slick clothes and imported shoes which had lace all over the place (it was rare then). They were (and still are) two of the most loving and simple guys we all have known. I have spent a lot of amazing times with each of these guys.

There is one more friend, with whom I go a very long way back. We have been friends since kindergarten. Aji has always been a very close friend. He didn't know the rest of the gang because from middle school, our schools were different, but he was always a constant in my life. He lived about 5 km away from my home and once we decided to start running in the morning, he had to come all the way to my home, wake me up and then take me running. When I got selected for the Navy, I decided to learn swimming and he decided to come along for support. When I say came along, he would come to my home at 5 am, jump over the locked gate, and get my mom or dad to open the door. Then he would come to my bedroom where I would be fast asleep, wake me up and then 'come along' with me to the pool. He has been like that throughout. I don't get to meet him as much as I like after he shifted to Dubai.

These were my closest friends while growing up. We spent a lot of time together. Their home was my home, and I could crash anywhere I wanted. I was never a guest and I am still considered and treated as part of their family. We meant what we spoke and there was no hidden agenda at any time. We were and still are always true to each other.

Good teachers are the reason why ordinary students dream of doing extraordinary things. I am one such ordinary student who, thanks to a great teacher, thought of looking beyond the everyday. Right from my middle school, I knew that I had to be part of the Indian Armed Forces, despite the fact that no one in my family had any armed forces background. The entire credit goes to one person—*Kiski*. *Kiski* what? No, it is *Kiski* who. He was my teacher from 5th grade all the way to 10th grade, Suresh Kumar sir. I don't think I ever knew why he was called *Kiski*. I am sure my friends must have shared the reason with me, but I don't remember. Speaking for myself, he was the best teacher I could have found. He won many state and national awards for being the best teacher, but all that happened much later. For us, he was our dear *Kiski*.

The interesting aspect about *Kiski*, other than the fact that he was one of the best teachers I had, was that he had joined the Indian Air Force and gone through their basic training. Unfortunately, he had to leave because of medical reasons. It didn't matter to him that he was not serving because his passion for the armed forces had rubbed off on me (it was a boring topic to others because he used to talk a lot about the armed forces). The seed for my dream to join the Air Force germinated in the small shed in front of his small house, which was our tuition centre. It had five wooden benches with three kids on each bench, and a roof made of coconut fronds. Sitting on the bench and listening to him speak about the armed forces, I was moved. I could see myself in those stories and anecdotes he shared. Interestingly, I don't think I mentioned even once to him that I wanted to join the Air Force. It was like a precious dream that I was holding close to my heart, known only to me. It was because of him that, I knew that I had to be part of the armed forces and the Air Force, specifically.

The cherry on the cake was when I discovered my sister's secret. I once found her secret album with photographs of her boyfriend who happened to be an Air Force pilot. I couldn't contain my excitement. I offered my whole-hearted support to them (not that they needed any from me) for the rest of my life. Suddenly, my dream looked more realistic to me as I had someone on the inside to talk about life in the armed forces. The more I knew and saw, the more dedicated and committed I became to my dream.

CHAPTER 2

THE SHIFT

I was preparing for the entrance exam for the National Defence Academy (NDA). It is one of the finest military institutions in the country where raw and young teenagers undergo rigorous training and grooming that transform them into gentlemen officers. One day, *Achan* showed me a newspaper advertisement for 10+2 (Tech) entry, inviting youngsters to join the Indian Navy as technical officers. It was called Naval Engineering Course or NEC. The entry would be based on the percentile score of my 12th exams. Then, there would be a screening test followed by the standard Service Selection Board (SSB) interview, which is the second toughest in the country after Civil Services. I dismissed it immediately saying that I wanted to be a fighter pilot and not some tech guy in the Navy. He said, 'It is better to get an experience of the interview before you go for your NDA interview.' It made sense to me and I boarded the train to attend the interview at SSB, Bhopal. My first trip out of Kerala, alone.

I did well in the aptitude test, thanks to all the aptitude tests that I used to solve from Competition Success Review, a magazine that *Achan* brought home dedicatedly for my sister who is nine years older than me. I don't think she ever attempted any of those, but I used to solve them even when I was in middle school because

I found them fascinating. Perhaps I was preparing myself for this aptitude test. Once I passed the test, I went in for the gruelling SSB interview which lasted a week. It took me through psychological evaluation, group tests, leadership challenges and much more, the most important being the personal interview. I managed to clear all of it with flying colours and was then sent for a medical examination that lasted another week. It was during my medicals that I found out that I needed spectacles. The number wasn't high, but it was enough to rule out my fighter pilot aspirations. I was clear that I did not want to join the Air Force in any other capacity. And that is how my Naval career started.

02 Dec 1991 is an unforgettable day for all of us who were in the course because that was the day when we all reported to the Naval Academy or NAVAC which was at INS[7] Mandovi at Goa (yes…Goa ☺). My first six-month training comprised a Naval orientation course there. NAVAC was situated right on top of a hill overlooking the sea. I could see the Arabian sea all around me and it was a dream coming true. Well, it was like that until my training started.

The first step after reporting is the most important—the haircut. I had a mullet that ran down to the bottom of my neck. I sat on the chair at the barber's and he asked me, 'Sir, how much time did it take for you to grow this hair?'

I proudly replied, 'About three to four months.'

He smiled and said, 'Just see what happens to it in the next three to four minutes.'

I didn't see any scissors there and I understood why in just three minutes. The whole process was over in three minutes sharp

---

[7]INS stands for Indian Naval Ship. All Naval ships and establishments are named with INS

and some who were waiting in line looked on in horror. I finished and started jogging towards my dormitory. I could feel the wind blowing and touching my skin just above my ears and I knew life was never going to be the same.

I had lived in Trivandrum all my life until then. I had a few friends who were very close and I lived in my happy world, composed of my family and friends.

All of a sudden, after my father left me at the academy, I was surrounded by strangers from different parts of the country, from different backgrounds and with different temperaments. The common thing amongst all of them was the fact that they were really good at whatever they did. All of them had that one thing the entire process of an SSB interview looks for. OLQ - Officer Like Qualities. Either you have it or you don't. You really need to have that X factor to get selected into the Armed Forces and all of them had it. Another common thing that all of us shared was the fact that we were scared. We didn't know what to expect and most of us were on our own for the very first time in our lives (except some hardcore ones from Sainik schools). Fear of the unknown, especially for a group of youngsters, is an excellent foundation for brotherhood and bonding with one another.

We soon learned that even though we were really good individually, we were clueless when it came to military training. It is always about the squadron and the division that we belonged to. Even punishments were hardly ever given individually. One person screws up, the whole squad suffers. So, we learned not just to look out for ourselves, but for each other as well. We had to make sure that everyone was on time for the 'fall-in' because if one was late, everyone was considered late. It became our default mode of functioning. Identify the ones who could not wake up on time, the ones who needed more time in the loo, or the ones who couldn't get the uniform done fast enough. Without even realizing it, we grew as a team, as a squad, as a division and as a squadron.

We not only learned about discipline, code of honour, and the importance of punctuality, but also about how to survive, how to sleep, that too standing upright, how to shave in the dark, and how to make our beds perfectly. Our parents would've been so proud to see us make our beds on our own, and also, how well we did it in under two minutes.

We learned drills and parades where individual excellence has no place at all. It is a great place to learn to work with others, to work up to expectations, not to overdo or show off, because the beauty of a marchpast is in the unison of the entire squad. The ones trying to show off were cut down to size and the ones not up to the mark were pulled up. The biggest incentive was that we had to do a perfect drill sequence individually to get permission to go on 'Liberty' – the one day when we got to step out of the confines of the Naval Academy to go explore Goa.

Of course, we could not wear anything we wanted, we had to wear a particular uniform called the *mufti* which was a trouser, a shirt and a tie. It was useful to stand out in the crowd and also avoid any seniors who also were out on the streets of Goa. We learned table manners in a crash course (read on the table in front of seniors). We learned how to eat almost every single thing that was put in front of us using a knife or spoon and a fork. I remember the trickiest being egg burji. We had to balance it on top of the fork and then put it into our mouths. Initially, I tried to push them and trap them between the lines of my fork. The only issue was that if my knife slipped, all that was supposed to go into the fork would land on the senior sitting opposite. That meant that I had to just close my plate and move out. Hunger is a great teacher. I learned quickly that it was smooth fingers and not brute force that helped me load the burji onto the fork.

Six months passed very quickly this way, because I did not have time to think of all that I left behind and the people who were part of my life. From hands-call at 0500h to lights out at 2200h, we were kept totally occupied and busy. The only reprieve was the classroom sessions where the instructor would teach a class and a few of us would force ourselves to be awake. The rest would be too exhausted to stay awake and listen to the lectures. I used this time to write letters to all my friends and family to keep my memories of them alive. It paid back well also because all of them responded with nice and long replies. The post used to come after lunch and the joy I felt every time my name was called to take a letter cannot be explained in words.

From swimming to gymnastics to cross-country, boxing, and dramatics to sailing, everything was a new skill learned at breakneck speed. We were too busy learning and getting into the groove to miss our homes and friends.

We had cross-country every Sunday. I wasn't a runner. The distance wasn't much. It was just about five to six kilometres. It started at the base of the hill (on top of which the Naval Academy was situated), which was great, but for some sadistic reason, the officers decided that it should not finish where it starts, but on the football ground inside the academy on top of the hill. Imagine doing the last half kilometre running up a hill which had a gradient closer to 45 degrees. I learned quickly that I didn't like running at all. The only motivator that pushed me forward was Liberty after cross-country.

One of the highlights of the orientation course at the Naval Academy was the camp 'Green Horn'. This really brought out the best and the worst in us. We were pushed to the edge to teach us to draw upon the last ounce of our physical, mental, and emotional reservoirs. This is where we really bonded as a team, we looked out for each other and drew upon each other's strengths. Just to reach the campsite, we had to do 20 km of boat-pulling followed by 20 km of running in the Full Scale Marching Order (FSMO) kit. After all this, the camp would start by pitching our tents, digging snake pits all around them, and setting up the tents in the best way possible. I don't think any of us were as bothered about snakes as being 'checked' for bad pits by our division officer.

Six months at the Naval Academy went by in a whirlwind of learning new skills, making friends, developing strong mindsets, and everything else that went into making me, well, an officer and a gentleman. I never realised how much I had changed even in physical appearance until I got down at the Trivandrum railway station after the initial training at NAVAC. *Amma* was desperately looking for me (I had given them my coach details). She walked towards me, looked at me for a few seconds, and to my utter shock, walked right past me, and continued to look for her son. I called out to her and she looked back. Her face changed and she started crying. Not because she couldn't recognise me, but because I had lost so much weight, had become darker (what did she expect?) and my voice had changed.

❊ ❊ ❊

After the orientation course at the Naval Academy, we went for a break of one month where my mother tried to get me back in 'shape' by feeding me all the time. This continues to date which irritates my sisters a lot (which I consider a bonus). They say the taste of what she prepares changes when I come home.

The remaining of my training, which was my B. Tech, was to happen at Naval College of Engineering at INS Shivaji, Lonavala. And our course was starting in June 1992. You should know something about Lonavala. It's a hill station next to Khandala where a lot of Bollywood movies, especially songs, are shot. It is situated between the two cities Mumbai and Pune, in the middle of Khandala ghats. The most interesting aspect about this place, other than being a hill station, is the fact that it is one the wettest places in India as it gets one of the highest rainfall every year. The monsoon starts in June, and you get to see the sun only in September/October. The raindrops are massive, and it hurts to stand in a full deluge. It is one of those places where it can rain 24 hours a day for weeks in a row. Well, it has its advantages as well. The place becomes picture-perfect during the monsoons. To head towards INS Shivaji, you need to take a deviation from Lonavala town. After about two kilometres, you would feel as if you have gone through a portal and entered a different world. You see the massive Tata dam in front of you. It looks like a huge lake with beautiful water. You are surrounded by lush green hills, and innumerable waterfalls that chill you and refresh you to the bone if you dare to stand under them. You soak in its breathtaking beauty and then you see the clouds. Not way up in the sky, but right in front of you, and you get to go through them. It is surreal when you do it for the first time.

The only way to truly enjoy Lonavala is to get soaked in the rain. Don't resist, don't fight, and don't be stupid enough to use an umbrella. Just embrace the rain with an open heart and body. Let the rain drench you, let the cold breeze send chills down to your bones. You start shivering with the rain and the breeze and then you stand by one of the many *dhabas*[8] along the road and have piping hot chai (tea) and *pakoras*[9]. It is magical. Every single one of my visitors to Lonavala swore that I was the luckiest person in the world to be able to live there.

But all this applies to visitors, not to the cadets doing their training. We don't even get the time to pause and enjoy the beauty of Lonavala until we become officers and do the last year of engineering. Well, in that one year, we make up for all the lost time as cadets. It's not that we did not enjoy it as cadets. It's just that we had so much stuff to do, our focus was never on the beauty of the place.

We lived in four dormitories as we were the junior-most batch. The four dorms were on the sides of what we fondly called the *Hard Patch*, which consisted of two basketball courts and a volleyball court. The hard patch holds so many fond memories. Let me just share that if it could speak, it would have quite the tale to tell. Whenever we, course mates meet even today, we always have a lot of stories to share about our *Hard Patch*. This was the place of action for us, especially junior cadets. Our day started with the command 'Delta Division Fall in'. I was in Delta division and 'fall-in' was the command to get the whole division into a squad before we started moving towards our destination. It could be for our physical training (PT), to the mess and even to our classes. Our days ended with the command '*Visarjan*' where the squad would turn half right and then dismiss and we retreated to our little heaven of the dorms. In reality, it looks more like rats scrambling back into the safety of their holes. A lot of our physical training, both by instructors as well as our seniors, the cool down after a cross-country, fierce

---

[8]A **Dhaba** is a roadside restaurant in the Indian subcontinent. They are on highways, generally serve local cuisine, and also serve as truck stops.
[9]A piece of vegetable or meat, coated in seasoned batter and deep-fried.

inter-division basketball and volleyball matches, tug of war and a whole lot of other competitions happened here. This was also the ideal place for punishments that were generously doled out by our training officers as well as seniors. As juniors, we had to live by some cardinal rules that a normal person might find funny or even weird. For example, we could never commit the crime of running across the hard patch (Yeah, we were not allowed to run across a concrete patch!). We had to run clockwise along the outermost side all the time. The smart ones who tried to cut across were at times considered brave (as it was their source of thrill and sense of achievement), but most of the time were just showered with the choicest swear words because invariably there would be some senior who would see it and as usual, the punishment was never for a single individual. I still don't know how someone from the senior course always managed to hide somewhere just to spring on us. The experiences on the hard patch were very painful at that time but are treasured now for the simple reason that nothing was ever done out of vengeance or malice. It shaped our minds more than our bodies to withstand and perform under really harsh conditions.

One side of the hard patch also had our coveted cadet's canteen. There was a small canteen which served tea and snacks for the cadets. It was meant for all, but as usual, all good things were 'out-of-bounds' for us in the first year. However, the unwritten rule that was always told to us was, 'Do anything, but don't get caught.' Some of my coursemates took this to heart and they really tested this theory. Unfortunately for the course, without much success in the beginning. One of the joys for us was when the canteen guy, who clearly understood our plight, used to come behind the dormitory with tea and snacks after pipe down. There was no proper light there and with whatever light we could get from the streetlights on the road to our new complex (where our seniors stay), he used to run his business. We used to gorge on cream rolls, samosas, and anything he had to offer. It was one guy handling some 20 to 30 odd, hungry and greedy (for the snacks) youngsters who also wanted to do it in the shortest time possible. We resembled cows chewing cud, but in sped-up motion. We would grab a cream roll(say) and run back to our beds and cover ourselves with the bedsheet. After a minute or so, one hand would slowly come up to our mouths and go back, followed by a minute of chewing. This was repeated till the entire cream roll vanished and we would sleep feeling on top of the world. While buying the snacks, some of us would pay first and then take the snacks and some others would take the snacks first to pay him later. This was a great opportunity for some business-minded guys who would take the cream roll from the fellow and later give it back and ask for their money back, which was never paid to him in the first place. Dorm stories are always very dear to us.

A little context into NEC. Naval Engineering Course was started as an experiment where youngsters were inducted after their 12th, and they were taught engineering while being cadets. It's never been done before, and we only have 25 courses or batches in total as part of this experiment. We consider ourselves quite elite because the experiment was so successful that it became the default entry into the Navy and the whole operation was shifted to Ezhimala in my own land, Kerala.

NEC was not as organised as NAVAC and definitely a far cry from NDA[10] because I was just in the 8th course which is equivalent to the 89th course of NDA. However, this very challenge became our strength. It was raw passion and drive that made NEC reach great heights. NEC was a speck in the vast base of INS Shivaji

---

[10] The National Defence Academy is the joint defence service training institute of the Indian Armed Forces, where cadets of the three services i.e., the Indian Army, the Indian Navy and the Indian Air Force train together before they go on to respective service academy for further pre-commission training

which was established as the premier technical training base for all Naval personnel since 1945. There were officers as well as sailors undergoing various training programs at any given time. INS Shivaji used to have close to 3000 officers and close to 8000 sailors every year in training. We were less than 300 in total, across three years in seniority. We had to compete with everyone else in all sports categories and that toughened us up all the way.

Life at NEC was tough. Seniors were tough but protective at the same time. There were a lot of responsibilities that were taken by the seniors who were our mentors who moulded us through their 'tough love'. They were a terrifying group for us. We couldn't hide anything from them. They were the 'all-seeing eye' for the NEC. There were literally no days when there was no punishment waiting for the squad for reaching late for a fall-in. Truth be told, it was a deliberate move by us. We knew that punishment was inevitable as they were pros at finding fault every time. Reaching early meant more time spent in punishment. It made more sense for us to reach late because dinner time was fixed, and punishments ended once the mess opened for dinner. We had one duty officer for the night. Some of them—actually, very few of them—were first-year friendly and the rest were senior-friendly. When someone in the latter group turned up for duty, we knew our nights would be long and tiring.

The weather didn't help us one bit in the process, especially the first term, more than half of which was during peak monsoons. We had to wear issued raincoats and headgear with long gum boots that came up all the way to the knee. Running in the gum boots was always difficult and as junior-most, we did not have the privilege to walk anywhere within the cadet's complex. . We had to jog, during PT, while going to the mess in uniform, while going to the class with a suitcase full of books in one hand and a heavy raincoat folded neatly in the other (in case it wasn't raining). The rains were wonderful for the initial two weeks. They reminded me of my hometown because of all the greenery around. Soon, things started getting difficult for all of us. We realised that none of our clothes dried properly and as days passed, the clothes started developing fungus on them. We had to continuously wash them to prevent that. Since all the clothes were hung on the lines that were common to all, the smart ones would just come and pick up whichever is dry and wear them, irrespective of who it belonged to. Most of the clothes never dried completely. We realised very soon that it was of no use to try and dry out our PT rig. PT fall-in happened at 0530h and the rains were incessant. It meant that the moment we stepped out of the dorms, we were drenched. We quickly got used to wearing wet PT rigs to make life easy.

One of the hallmarks of the NEC was its cross-country. Our cross-country run was about 16 kilometres every Sunday morning. No amount of rain or storm could keep it from happening. As the junior-most squad, we were not used to running such long cross-country. Therefore, to teach us and to acclimatize us, our evening sports time was converted into practice sessions for cross-country. We ended up running shorter versions of cross-country almost every day. We had no choice but to learn the art of running long distances. We learned to get into a rhythm, and run in step during practice runs. At times, we even enjoyed it. This mostly depended on the senior who was taking us for these runs. Our cross-country started at Shivaji cadet's football ground. We had to run all the way to Tata dam, then turn and run all the way back. This also meant that the cross-country route, during monsoons was beautiful. As mentioned earlier, we were surrounded by hills and thanks to the continuous rains, there were waterfalls, small and large, everywhere. There were times when we would run through mist and clouds as they were all around us. Even in the middle of all the pain, I couldn't help but marvel at the beauty we were surrounded by. During our practice runs, if the senior was an enterprising one, half-way through the run, we were given the gift of standing under one of the many waterfalls. I have never experienced anything as refreshing to date. All the tiredness and fatigue used to vaporize in the freshness of the chilled water falling all over us. We really had to learn how to run with the right technique because we were issued with old canvas shoes which had absolutely no cushioning. We had to master the perfect way of rolling our feet while running so that there was no impact on our legs. Those who didn't learn it, ended up with stress fractures.

Sometimes I feel that maybe some of them did it deliberately to get away from the daily punishments. The most rewarding words that we aspired to get from the sick bay was 'Excuse PPG', which means Excused from PT, Parade and Games. But our seniors knew how to make even that a horror. After all, they had gone through the same things that we were going through, and they knew exactly what was going on in our minds.

There are enough stories from my first year that can fill this book. Very interesting ones (which didn't feel so that time) that we fondly recall whenever there is a course get-together. In short, we learned discipline, bonded as one unit, and competed with each other in divisional games, among many other things. One division comprised of about 32 cadets across three years of seniority and from these 32, we had to cough up two teams: string 1 and string 2. So, we all ended up doing everything together every time. There was no excuse for anyone. Those who were not very good at sports (like me) ended up in string 2 and the leftovers (if any) were the cheer group. We had to be everywhere when our team played. NEC taught us the perfect *Esprit de Corps* through brute force. If we were cheering, we literally had to lose our voices by the end of the match.

The saddest part was that the NEC entry was once a year unlike the NDA, which meant that we did not become seniors in six months. We had to wait an entire year, across two semesters, to become seniors.

I still remember when we came back after the first-semester leave. People started reaching the railway station by evening and we were all huddled in one place where the Shaktiman[11] trucks for INS Shivaji would pass. We were supposed to catch one of the trucks and head back to our cadet's complex. Every time one such truck passed, one of us would say, 'Please stop the truck' and someone would call out in the softest voice to the truck driver, who obviously wouldn't hear it. It kept happening until the last truck came and we had no choice but to pile ourselves into it and head back for another six months of being the junior-most batch.

CHAPTER 3

A SPIRITUAL ESCAPADE

The best thing about being a second-year cadet was that we finally had juniors! Well, it was one of the best things because there were a couple of them. To start with, we had our own rooms in the cadet's block (such luxury)! It was both good and not-so-good for us because this also meant that we were right next to our seniors who were in their third year. My room comprised one bed, one study table and chair, and one steel locker. That was my world for the remaining two years. The bed was my refuge, at least until the attack of bed bugs. Trust me, there is really no respite from them. I ended up sleeping on the floor with my mattress leaving the entire bed to the bugs.

We could also walk (well, march) from place A to place B. We could actually touch our hands on the table while we ate. We could sit back and take the support of the backrest instead of sitting on the edge of the chair with erect spines. We also got more time for each meal. From five minutes for breakfast and seven minutes for lunch (on our worst days), we could utilize the entire 20 to 30 mins with no one scrutinising our every move.

As soon as the juniors arrived, some of us rolled up our sleeves to pounce on them. There were never any ill thoughts or vengeance or malice of any kind. The fact is that when you want to take charge of a junior, you must be mentally prepared to go through the grind yourself. For example, if you called a junior to report to you at 0500h, it meant that you had to be up and ready before that. Some of my friends got into that role very easily. Some of us stayed back and interacted with juniors only on a need-to basis. I felt that the rigours that they had to go through were tough enough, and also, there were enough josh parties to 'look after' the juniors.

It was also a great feeling to be responsible for grooming them throughout the year. As said in the movie *Spiderman*, 'With great power comes great responsibility.' We could terrify the juniors inside the complex, but the moment we stepped out, we became their guardians. There was a cardinal rule (at least during my time) that if you are with a senior, you are not supposed to touch your wallet. Everything gets 'taken care of' by the senior accompanying you. It could be for a short official trip outside the base, or it could be the journey back home at the end of the term. So, I would say that things were balanced overall.

Even though I had become a senior, there was no respite from cross-country every Sunday morning. Thankfully, we did not have to do the practice runs almost every day like we did in our junior year, and we had enough cross-country enthusiasts who were more than willing to take our juniors for their daily practice. Cross-country, for me, was like an anti-climax because, on Saturdays, we used to have movie nights. We would go to the theatre and get lost in the beautiful world of Bollywood or Hollywood movies. I used to get transported into their world and revel in it. At the end of the movie, I would get up from the seat with the sinking feeling that I had to run the next morning, and that too, 16 km. If you are a marathon runner, you must be thinking how lucky I was to get into running at such an early age. With all due respect, please understand that there are people like me who don't like running and are still perfectly happy. I do run even now owing to health reasons for just a few kilometres. Anyway, most of the time, our Sunday cross-country runs used to start from the football ground. While I used to stand there dreading the start whistle, I used to look around. Our football ground was flanked on two sides by the wardroom or officers' mess (where I would be living just after two more years). I could see young officers who graduated the previous year sitting on the windowsill with a cup of coffee in hand watching us start the cross-country. I wanted to do that oh-so-much. I just wanted to get up early on a Sunday morning, pick up my coffee and realize that I didn't have to run (yay). On top of it, I would be able to see cadets lined up (like I was) for the Sunday cross-country. Yeah, one of the cheap thrills that I was looking forward to, once I completed the course. In retrospect, when I finally did complete the course, I preferred to sleep in rather than gawk at freshers so early on a Sunday morning!

The fact is that whether anyone liked it or not, in NEC, we ran a lot. Even with our combined strength of less than 300 as NEC cadets, we had to compete with other established military institutions in various sports and games competitions like Hexagonals where six cadet training academies come together to compete. Institutions like the NDA had more than 300 cadets in just one term of six months, and they had cadets across six terms. Naturally, the talent pool was way bigger there. Despite that, when it came to cross-country, no one could beat us. NEC was driven more by our killer spirit when it came to cross-country and other sports.

We took pride in our running, and it rubbed off on everyone, even those like me. I learned that when it came to doing things for the division or our beloved NEC, personal likes and dislikes always took a backseat. This is one common trait that is cultivated across the entire armed forces and this same spirit comes up and helps our soldiers face the toughest enemies, braving all odds. If we were motivated so much to do for our division or academy, how much more would we be able to do for our beloved country? This has stayed with me throughout my life—the lesson that I should always look beyond myself and work towards the greater good rather than hide behind my limitations and preferences.

I have always been a spiritual person. I was born in a Hindu family and lived in a lane which had a lot of Christian families who were very close friends. There were five houses in the lane, and all were Christian families except for us. We were all like one big family and the icing on the cake (literally) was that we always got four cakes and other sweets during Christmas. Every year, my parents used to send me to VBS (Vacation Bible School) which used to happen in the church during our school holidays. It served two purposes for my parents. Firstly, it definitely taught me a lot of good things and helped me work on my character and morality, and the second, which I believe was more critical for them was to keep me engaged for at least half a day so that they had time to breathe and finish other works without having to worry about me. I also used to go with all the other kids to watch 'Christian movies' that were screened regularly in the church that was less than 100m from my home. It was basically a slide show where one slide would be shown, and the priest would share the incident or story associated with the picture. Moving to the next slide was an event in itself. The priest would rise to the tip of his toes and extend his right hand above his head and then in one sweeping action would bring his hand across the slide all the way to the bottom. This elaborate action was an indication to the projector guy who was just a few feet away from him to move to the next slide. I don't remember any of the slides or the stories today, but I vividly remember the priest and his actions. It was a very friendly and cordial atmosphere at the church where the priest knew everyone. In fact, the first time I ever went on stage was for an event in this church. I was Jesus and I remember someone putting some kind of gum all over my face and putting powdered charcoal (that we used for brushing our teeth when we went to our native places) all over my face to give me the 'beard'.

As a family, we always believed in the goodness of people and never looked at anyone based on their faith. I was always willing to learn and adopt the best practices from anything, be it a religion, a lecture, or a seminar. I always had fond memories of VBS, and I always used to carry a small Bible with me, even though I never even attempted to read anything from it. I had carried the same to NEC as well.

In the seniors' block, there were two rows of rooms, facing each other. I had a very dear mallu friend, Harish Pillai, staying opposite me. We were very close friends and like most of my other close friends, he also called me 'Beems'. One evening, during our free time, I went to say hello to Harish, and I saw him reading a huge Bible. I told him I also have one and showed him the miniature one that was kept under my pillow. He casually asked me if I wanted to know more about Jesus and I told him what I have always told many people who tried to tell me that Jesus is the only saviour and I need to believe only in him. I said, 'I would like to know more but just don't try to convert me. I respect your beliefs and I expect you to do the same with me.' He smiled and told me not to worry. He asked me to accompany him during the weekend to his home in Pune, which later became my home as well.

We reached his home on Sunday and after lunch, he took me to meet an elderly lady. She had hair white as snow and sparkling eyes. Harish introduced me to Aunty Jade who was his mentor and spiritual guide. I really do not remember the conversation we had, but at the end, she asked me if I would like to accept Jesus into my life and I said, 'Yes.' I still don't know why I said yes. She made me repeat a short prayer inviting Him and something happened at the end of the prayer. I cannot rationally or logically explain the experience, but I had changed. Totally and completely. Deep in my Spirit, I knew this was the truth. I felt calm and complete. I had entered her home saying I will not be converted, and I came out declaring that I was a Believer.

Today, after decades, I have reached a neutral place where I do not deny either Jesus or any of the Hindu scriptures. This happened because of some other life experiences that I went through more than a decade later. I went through different lifetimes of mine, during a hypnotherapy session which is in total contradiction to what the Bible says. However, I cannot deny the experiences that I had in both cases. So now, I follow Hinduism and rituals, but I do not think twice to attend a Sunday service and worship if I get the chance.

From that day at Aunty Jade's home, my life changed all over again. All weekends were spent in Pune at Harish's home and Aunty Jade's place studying the Bible. We were 'born-again' Christians who strictly followed the Bible (the word of God) and didn't believe in God having any physical representations – be it churches, the image of Jesus or even a cross for that matter because the Bible says that God is a Spirit, and we should only worship him in Spirit and truth. Even though this did cause quite a heartburn to both my family as well as Harish's, they were quite alike in their thought processes where they gave priority to us being good human beings more than what faith or belief we practised. This was a major turning point in my second year at NEC and I remained an uncompromising believer for over a decade. I did not know at that time that this would lead to some major life events. Some very bad and some very good.

There were several other incidents in my second year of training as well. A lot of them were very funny when I look back. Finally, I went into the third and final year of my cadet life. I started looking forward to and dreaming about life as an officer at the end of the year.

CHAPTER 4

THE TRUTH IS... SUBJECTIVE?

In the final year, we have all the privileges that a cadet can have in NEC. We hardly interact with the first-year cadets because we were the 'grand-pops' and if they did something seriously wrong, their 'pops' or the second-year cadets had to bear the brunt of it. The relationship with our immediate juniors also changed to being friendly unless there was some massive issue. It would have been a peaceful and memorable year if one particular issue had not happened halfway through. We were having our midterm exams and we had our study periods in between. What I have written about the rigours of the NEC is just about 10% of what actually happens. You must remember that we were doing our B. Tech in the middle of all this. Yeah, it was a deadly combination. No regular engineering student would be able to handle even a fraction of all that we went through. It is by design as a military engineer's life can never be compared to a normal engineer's life outside. We had to gear ourselves up to tackle technical issues while living the military life. It was only during exam time that we had a lot of leeway for our studies. We even had PT and games suspended during exams.

What happened was that one third-year cadet was taking charge of a second year and the junior reacted physically. You must understand that one of the things that are strictly forbidden in the armed forces is any kind of physical violence, especially towards a junior. That falls under ragging. The fact was that when we were the junior-most, our seniors used to rap us now and then and we did not think much of it because, for us, it was like our parents rapping us for something that we did grossly wrong. We knew that there was no vengeance or malice in their acts. For me, the intent is far more important than the act and we all knew the intent was pure.

I guess the junior batch didn't see it that way, at least one junior definitely did not, which is also fair because that is what the rulebook said. Well, to cut the long story short, what I heard (I was not present to know what really happened) was that one third-year cadet rapped a junior and while trying to get away from it, the third-year cadet's hand landed on the junior's lips which got cut. On top of it, I was told that the junior caught hold of the third-year's hand.

Now, this was something unheard of. Even when we had issues with seniors, we could not even in our wildest dreams think of getting physical with our seniors. Maybe because how we saw them was totally different. Well, these days, I do hear about even children getting physically aggressive with their parents. Something similar happened here as well.

This created a hue and cry among us third-years. It was like throwing a stone at the hornet's nest. All of us came out of our rooms where we were studying and took the entire batch to the task. One section of our batch had lab exams. So, they were nowhere in the scene. When we came out, we saw the entire junior course doing push-ups. Someone even told me that the 'nice' seniors like me also should get involved so that they realize this is something serious. We all got involved and made sure that they were doing it right and rapped the ones who were not doing it right. I remember vaguely that I had asked two of them to stand up, rapped them lightly and told them to do push-ups properly. It was all about driving home an important message that many things can be accepted but getting physical with a senior will never be tolerated.

I went back to my room after about 15 minutes and the punishment lasted for another 20 to 30 minutes after which they were sent back for their studies since it was exam time. What happened after that was something that we wouldn't think of doing in our wildest dreams. The junior who was at the receiving end decided to use the pen. He wrote a written complaint against all of us and submitted it to the office.

Well, it was another hornet's nest that was stirred. An official complaint is treated very seriously, especially when it indicates any kind of ragging. The policy is very clear regarding that. By evening muster, the whole place was swarming with every officer who was attached to the cadet training department. I guess they also wanted to convey a similar message to the one we tried to convey to our juniors.

The juniors were asked to give statements about what happened and who were involved. The juniors gave the names of a few of us who, according to them, had been troubling them all through the year or those who they felt lacked compassion and empathy. The next step was to form a Board of Enquiry (BOE) into the incident. Even though we were cadets, we were gentlemen cadets or people of officer's stature. Officers are always tried through a BOE. This was led by a Commander from INS Shivaji itself. They questioned the juniors as well as the ones whose names were mentioned by them. I guess by then, even the junior who gave the complaint did not want things to escalate to this level. After all, this can ruin someone's career. Maybe he wanted to just give us a jolt and did not foresee the events this whole incident had snowballed into.

Fortunately for us, the officers who were from the base understood the real situation on the ground and maybe they realised that the intent of the complainer was not to ruin their senior's life or career. They concluded the BOE and sent their findings to the Southern Command, under which comes all training establishments irrespective of where they were located geographically.

But the Commander-in-Chief there had a different set of ideals (good or bad is a matter of perspective). He rejected the findings of the board that conducted the enquiry, and he sent an external team led by a Commodore. Well, the Commanding Officer of our base, INS Shivaji, was also of the same rank. We realised that this whole incident had taken a very serious turn.

Meanwhile, back in the cadet's complex, right at the start, we decided to take *Esprit de Corps* to the next level. We felt that if only a few names were there (the ones given by juniors), they would be made examples of (read specimens) and we felt that all of us needed to be in this together. So, every single person who was involved in the incident, no matter what role, gave statements on their own. The first board did not even consider these statements because there were no complaints against them.

The new BOE team took all statements into consideration, and they started their deliberations and interviews with everyone concerned. There was genuine tension around everyone who was involved in the incident. I asked every single person who went for the interview if he spoke the truth, the entire truth. Everyone promised me that they had shared everything and did not hold back anything.

For me, there is only one version of the truth. It was black or white for me and I came from a group of friends who spoke the absolute truth. I never had to read between the lines. That was who I was. That is who I am even today.

They kept calling people one by one and my turn came towards the very end. I went in there and I could see that they were visibly tired from this month-long process of listening to everyone and taking notes. The senior-most officer instructed the team to ask me three questions and gave the question numbers. It was a very simple process. Name and personal details, whether I was present during the incident and finally, 'Explain what happened'. Simple instructions, right?

The ball was in my court. No one had given my name. They did not have anything against me. I explained what happened that day—that I had come down to have tea, heard the commotion, saw the juniors doing push-ups and I ensured that they were doing it properly and after a while, I left to go back to my room. This was the truth, but not the whole truth according to me. It was a white lie, and I could easily get away with that. My mind was racing. I was thinking to myself that I need to be truthful, especially since every person I had spoken with had assured me that they had spoken the whole truth. I had to make a decision on the spot. I had to choose between my value system, not letting my coursemates down and getting away with what I had done. My conviction about my value system won in that split second and even though they had finished my interview, I added just one more line. 'Sir, during the time I was there, I slapped two cadets.'

The entire atmosphere changed over there. Others who were doing their work stopped it and came and sat in front of me. It was like one of those moments in comedy sitcoms when you do something really stupid and the whole cast looks at you for a moment and pauses before breaking up into loud laughter. Well, from the look and the pause in front of me, I knew that something had gone seriously wrong. After the pause, there was a barrage of questions. Who did I slap? I honestly didn't know. It was just a couple of random juniors who were not doing push-ups properly and it was just one slap, not even a hard one. They said, 'How can you not know who they were, unless you were slapping everyone? You specifically said two cadets. Tell us their names.'

My mind had gone blank by then. I was only wondering if I had made the biggest blunder with that statement. I mumbled two names that I knew (afterwards when I checked with them, they clearly told me that I had not even touched them). They were also called for interviews, and they told them the truth. Well, it didn't matter anymore. I had confessed to a crime. After I went back, I analysed the scenario, and I realised that I had to tell the truth. Otherwise, I wouldn't have been able to live knowing that I did not tell the truth, that I may have let down my coursemates who had spoken the truth.

The board went back with their findings. Weeks and months passed, and the news was slow to trickle in. Two of us from the batch might get expelled, some others would lose a year (relegation) and the rest would get seniority-cut. I was kind of happy knowing that I would get seniority-cut. After all, I deserved it for playing a small part in the whole incident. We later came to know that they took expulsion out of the equation, and we even knew the names of the six people who were getting relegated. Those were the people whose names were put up by the juniors.

Final exams got over and we were preparing for our final holidays. We were to come back after the holidays and then graduate as officers. We could hardly contain our excitement. One day, we were sitting in the classroom when our training commander walked into the room. He had the official confirmation of the result of the BOE. He said, 'Following cadets are relegated and they have to conjoin with the junior course.'

He read out six names. The seventh was mine. He read one more name, but my mind had gone blank by then. I didn't cry. I just sat there totally numb. It took me a few minutes to get my senses back. Once I did, my first question was to find out who the eighth cadet was. Someone shared the name with me. I got up and went to him and asked him point-blank. 'What did you tell them during the interview?' He had done exactly the same that I had done.

I called home that night and told my parents that I had lost a year. I was expecting a backlash, but my father only asked me whether it meant that I was expelled from the Navy. I told him no and he said, 'Not to worry, you have lost just a year, it's not the end of your life or career. Don't take it to heart.'

Those words gave me so much assurance and faith in myself and at that moment, standing inside the STD booth, I broke down. I had not cried until that moment. I was in shock trying to process everything that happened. I was sure that my parents would be totally disappointed in me. My friends would become officers in a month, and I just didn't know what I would do. Everything was weighing on my mind but the biggest and the heaviest was the fact that I had let my parents down. When *Achan* dismissed this entire event as a minor one, I initially did not know how to react. Then I realised how much those words meant to someone who was surrounded by dark clouds and a storm in every direction. I had concluded that it was the end of the road for me and there was nothing to look forward to. However, *Achan*'s words of reassurance woke me up from the trance that I was caught in. Once I was out of shock, I was able to give vent to the full range of my emotions. I cried silently all the way back to my room and once in the room, I cried myself to sleep.

Once all the emotions that were pent-up inside me were dealt with, I was able to think more clearly and logically. For the first few days, I was furious with my coursemates who had lied to me about being truthful. We were all equally guilty of what we had done. I felt that they let me down completely. Those few days were horrible.

At one point, I realised that everyone else was going about their lives as usual and I was the only one sitting with a bitter heart. It was like me drinking poison and expecting other people to die. This condition was not serving me at all. I had to do something. So, I decided to question my beliefs for my own peace and well-being.

My biggest concern was the betrayal. I am not someone who would ever betray anyone, let alone my friends and coursemates. I had to really push myself to question the biggest concern. The conversation went something like this.

Me1: They betrayed me.

Me2: Really? Did they really betray you?

Me1: Of course, they did because I asked them whether they spoke the truth and they all said yes to me.

Me2: Hmm. What is truth to you?

Me1: What do you mean? There is only one truth. The absolute truth. It is either black or white.

Me2: Well, is it possible that everyone does not share your definition of truth?

Me1: Yes.

Me2: Is it also possible that in their minds they did speak their truth and therefore did not lie to you when they said they spoke the truth?

Me1: Yes (in a feeble voice. I could not refute the logic that was being presented to me).

Me2: Therefore, is it also possible that they did not betray you?

Me1: Yes.

Me2: Is it important for you to uphold your values, in this case, about what is the truth to you?

Me1: Yes.

Me2: Then are you upset that you spoke the truth?

Me1: Definitely not. I would not have been able to live with myself otherwise.

Me2: If you decide to live by your values, there will be consequences like this. So, you need to decide here. Do you still want to hold on to your value system?

Me1: Yes.

Me2: Why?

Me1: That is my identity. If I let go of my value system, I will have nothing left in me.

Me2: So, are you willing to take responsibility for your actions? Both during the incident as well as during the interview?

Me1: Yes (this time feeling much better).

Me2: Now comes the most important question. WHAT NEXT?

I don't want to be pompous and say that this was an easy conversation. I did not want to have this conversation. I wanted to hide behind my blame game. I wanted to hate my coursemates. I wanted to hate my juniors because of whom I lost a year.

I tried to do that for a while, but it was not helping. I was becoming a person whom I did not like at all. It was a very awkward situation. The relationship between seniors and juniors is very different when it comes to the armed forces and especially during cadet training years. My juniors were feeling bad that the whole thing turned out like this. My coursemates were feeling bad that they would have to leave me behind when they moved into the wardroom. I was caught in a web of my own emotions which were destructive.

One day, not long after this incident, I decided to address this as well. I took a book and wrote on top WHAT NEXT. I had to find a way out of this mental and emotional state I was struggling in. I knew that the way I was seeing things was not right because I was feeling very low.

I started listing the consequences of losing a year. These were the thoughts that were going on in my mind and weighing me down. I knew that I had to find positives in each of these.

1. I have to repeat all the studies for a year.
   - That meant that I would be repeating what I have already studied. It would be much easier this time and I will have more time to do something else.

2. I have to spend an entire year with my juniors as one of them.
   - I was always liked by my juniors. They will welcome me with both arms.
3. There are still a lot of pent-up emotions inside me.
   - I can channel them by focusing on something that would consume me. (That is how I picked up a guitar and guess who was my teacher? One of the juniors whose name I had given for slapping. He became such a great friend all through that year and remains one to date.)
4. I have to run one more year of cross-country.
   - Ah, well, I still cannot find a way to flip this. I had to apply something that I learned during my *'Ultimate Leadership Certification Camp'* from an ex-sergeant of the US Military who trained us. When things got tough, his favourite line was *'Suck it up, Princess.'* Even though I heard this decades later, this is exactly what I did for that one year when it came to cross-country runs every week.

Looking back at this entire incident, I can say with conviction now that it was one of the best things that ever happened to me. My entire life trajectory changed because of this incident.

WHAT I LEARNED FROM THIS INCIDENT:

1. Just because I hold certain values close to my heart, doesn't mean that everyone around me also has the same values.
2. Definitions of things vary from person to person. In my case, it was about truth. It could be with anything else. I stopped expecting others to adhere to *my* definition of things that are dear to me.
3. My mental and emotional state is totally in my hands. Not anyone else's. It is all up to me.

4. Other people respond to the way I perceive them. If I had seen my coursemates as people who betrayed me, I would have lost more than 60 friends (yeah, our batch size was big) who are like brothers today.
5. The faster I got my mind away from the incident and all the associated emotions, the faster I could move forward.
6. If I look for positives in any situation, I will find it.
7. There will be some things where I just have to say, 'Suck it up' and move forward. I may not get answers to everything all the time.
8. When something bad happens, find a way to dissipate my energy and emotions by doing something constructive (in my case it was learning to play the guitar).
9. And always ask, WHAT NEXT?

CHAPTER 5

THE LOWEST FORMS OF MARINE LIFE

Being an officer in the Navy is not just a matter of pride. It is also pretty cool, especially when you are young and in the prime of life. I couldn't call myself the 'happening guy', though. Even though I had the potential, I did not have the mindset. I was more of an introvert, the quintessential, mind-my-own-business kind. Technically, I was in the Lonavla–Pune–Mumbai belt and I had double the number of coursemates, (thanks to me losing a year,) and most of them had a very active and colourful social life thanks to the fact that Pune was full of students who considered young Naval officers to be cool. To top it off, coursemates are always more than willing to help a fellow coursemate who did not have a date or a partner for the disc during weekends. Despite such support and opportunities all around, I chose to be mostly homebound because I found my home-away-from-home in Pune through Harish's family. It may have deprived me of getting many 'hits' with the opposite sex, but the time spent with Harish, Amma and Lak (will tell you more about them soon) is one of my cherished memories not just of my training years, but forever.

I finished my B. Tech at NEC by Aug 1997 and the next part of the program was MESC (Marine Engineering Specialization Course). This was a two-year program which had many different courses in it. One of the most exciting parts was doing watchkeeping on board a ship for six months. Now, watchkeeping is one of the most important parts of any Engineer Officer's career. We must keep watch of the engine room of the ship (since I chose to be a Marine Engineer instead of Electrical Engineer) for a certain number of hours every day. We mostly had a 3-watch system[12] to ensure that all the personnel were optimally utilised. There is always one officer in charge of the engine room during the watch. A watchkeeping certificate basically states that this officer is competent enough to handle the ship's engine room during a 'watch' on his own.

This also meant another thing. When we started as cadets, especially in the first year, our seniors used to sneer at us and call us the 'lowest form of marine life' and some of the enthusiastic duty officers would call the entire cadet fraternity (which included our seniors also) the same. This always caused some of the senior-most cadets to squirm and us, the junior-most, to feel happy. From being small fish in a small pond, we had struggled for years to become the biggest fish in the very same pond.

From there, we jumped straight into the ocean (no gradual progression through larger ponds) and we again became the lowest form of marine life in the operational Navy. From senior-most cadets back to the junior-most officers. It didn't matter much because officers are always treated like officers and when you come from a place like the NEC, there is nothing worse you could experience in life (or so I thought). The only disadvantage

---

[12] A 'watch' is somewhat like a 'shift' at a factory or other manufacturing activity. 'On Watch' is Navy talk for doing your job on your shift. In a 3 watch system, the 24 hours gets divided into 3 parts and they are named Red, Blue and White.

of being the junior-most officer was that we used to get DTV. Not dish TV. We call it *'Detailed to Volunteer'*. Whenever some events were happening at the command level, volunteers were asked to attend from each ship and as the junior-most, we were the default 'volunteers' for all the uninteresting events.

The ship that I got posted for doing my watchkeeping was INS Vindhyagiri which was in the Eastern Naval Command. It was a Nilgiri class frigate that was commissioned in 1981. Even after 16 years, she was in pretty good shape. She is no more now (decommissioned) and went out, unfortunately, not in a memorable way. I will always have fond memories of my time on board. I guess most of us would share similar sentiments about our watchkeeping tenure. This was the first time we were posted on a ship. A true-blue Indian warship. The Navy is all about the ships. The Naval fleet. Every other organization, whether it's the training centres, dockyards, schools, colleges and even the headquarters, exists to support the fleet. I was on board one of them. The pride I felt was totally at another level.

I was posted along with one of my original coursemates, Munish (who also lost a year due to the same incident). Watchkeeping can be pretty gruelling, and it really helps if you have a good buddy with you. Munish and I were close friends by then. He was one of the academic toppers in the course. He had helped me a lot with my academics especially during one of the exam weeks when I was bedridden due to a fever. He came to my room, sat next to me on my bed and taught me for the exam of the next day.

I had even gone with him in one of our term breaks to his home to meet his family. That is another trip that I will remember forever. His family was the epitome of love and care with his dad who had retired from the Air Force, his mom, and his sister, who was also an officer in the Indian Airforce. She had taken leave during his break so that they all could be together as a family. A true-blue *fauji*[13] family. They loved each other a lot and it was very visible. They immediately adopted me also as one of theirs. It was all laughter, music, conversations, and food throughout. Even though I had not planned to visit any places there or had even expressed any desire to do so, they took it up as a family mission to help me explore the place as well as enjoy all the north Indian cuisines. I was there just for a couple of days, but they took me around the city and explained everything around there. We visited the Rock Garden which is a very famous as well as beautiful place to visit. It is a 40-acre marvel that is made up of multi-coloured art pieces and sculptures. You will never see a more beautiful use of waste material anywhere. All the creations were from broken bottles, glasses, tiles, ceramic pots, ceramic pieces and even broken toilets. The biggest surprise for me was to know that it was built single-handedly by one person who was a PWD[14] officer, in his spare time.

Another visit was up the hills where we went in their car and reached the Timber trail rope way at Parwanoo. The rope way was across two hills going all the way up to 5000 ft. The ride is about two km and takes about 15 to 20 minutes to complete. We had sandwiches and other snacks packed with us and we started early from home. Just the ride to and from there was such a happy one. I had never been on a ropeway in my life before and it was an amazing experience. My heart still fills with happiness and love every time I recall the days that I spent with them. They just poured all their love and affection on me and fed me an assortment of mouth-watering North Indian dishes. They all laughed heartily for at least a minute when I was aghast at the information that they made rotis with

---

[13]Slang for a military person
[14]Public Works Department – A government organisation

'*makhi*'. I didn't realize that they were not making the rotis with '*makhi*' which meant flies in Hindi, but with '*makki*' which meant corn in Punjabi. Makki di roti is a delicacy in the north, especially in winter. I headed to my hometown after a couple of days of their amazing hospitality. It was truly a trip to remember.

Munish and I landed on INS Vindhyagiri for our six months of watchkeeping. We were nervous as we were back to being the junior-most and it was our first experience on board an operational ship. The Engine Room department consisted of three officers. The HOD was Commander Pradeep Bahri and his designation on board was Commander(E). He was a very stylish man with a thick moustache and hair and a thorough gentleman with a good sense of humour. His English was impeccable and was very articulate in his speech. He was also very good at his craft and had done his M. Tech from IIT. He was not the nosy, overbearing, micro-managing type and gave us the freedom to learn and grow.

Next was our Senior Engineer, Lieutenant Commander Suryakant Redekar. He was kind of opposite to what Commander(E) was when it came to looks and speech. He mostly spoke Hindi and his English was like mine—basic. He was very raw in his approach and interactions even though he was equally loving and caring towards us. We never saw him without a smile. I don't really remember seeing him in anything other than his white dungarees[15] while we were on board. He was working all the time. He was assisted by an Assistant Engineer Officer, Lieutenant Harish. He looked more like a Telugu film star with the typical thick moustache and stylish hair. Interestingly, it turned out that he was indeed from Andhra and was from an affluent family. He always wore fashionable clothes when off the ship and had a very stylish and powerful bike. He was more like a friend and guide to us throughout our tenure there.

---

[15]Overalls that are worn during working on board the ship, especially by the technical department. Officers wear white ones and sailors wear blue ones.

The ship was based in the Eastern Naval Command, which was at Vishakhapatnam. I had come from the hustle and bustle of Mumbai where we had to do some short courses prior to our watchkeeping. We used to call ourselves *Lonavla ke pahadi*[16] *log* When I was in Mumbai for the first time, the purposefulness of the people and the general pace of life in the city were culture shocks for me. It was the first time I experienced something like that in my life.

Remember that my origins are from Kerala, God's own country, where time stands still. This is a place where you can watch a five-minute sunset for hours. It is all very poetic and romantic and all, but after a point, it can be frustrating. Everyone has time in Kerala and if you go to a junction anywhere in the state, you will always find a group of people in front of a '*chaya kada*', the veritable Kerala teashop, making small talk with everyone around, discussing the latest policies of American presidents and how the current government (irrespective of which party is ruling) is ineffective and of course, how Sachin Tendulkar should be batting.

In comparison to Kerala and even Lonavla, Mumbai appeared cold and indifferent to me initially. You need to, at least once in your life, stand at Churchgate or CST[17] station and watch the crowds there, especially during office traffic. You will find a million people descending from a local train that is built to hold just a fraction of them. You will not see anyone who is lost, not sure what to do or not know where to go. No one has time for chitchat (they do loads of it during their commute). Once they get down, they head straight to where they are supposed to go. No time to 'hang around'. I used to think that maybe Mumbaikars were indifferent.

---

[16]Pahadi, broadly refers to **people from Uttarakhand and Himachal Pradesh,** who claim themselves to be the rightful inhabitants of the Himalayas.
[17]Chhatrapati Shivaji Terminus

Nothing could be further from the truth. You can ask anyone who has stayed a few years in Mumbai, and they will swear that when they reached Mumbai from another city, they hated the city but after a couple of years, they could not imagine living anywhere else. I have experienced this to some extent as my lovely wife was born and brought up in Mumbai. So, I have known the frustration of leaving Mumbai first-hand. To summarize, Mumbai grows on you and once you have lived there, you cannot imagine living anywhere else.

Vizag (aka Vishakhapatnam) was the city that would give me some of the best and worst that life had to offer. The place reminded me of Kerala to some extent. It did not have the full extent of the natural beauty of Kerala, but it had plenty of beautiful beaches. To give you some perspective, people of my generation or older know of a famous Bollywood movie called *Ek Duje Ke Liye* and one of the hallmarks of the movie was beaches. Most of them were in Goa but the iconic song '*Tere Mere Beech Mein*' was shot in Gangawaram Beach in Vizag. There were many beaches like that and some of them used to be our ship's picnic spots. Vizag was not as slow as Kerala, but it was way slower than Mumbai. It so happens that the slowness of Vizag also grows on you. I have spoken to many naval families who came from Mumbai to Vizag and transitioned all the way from 'Man, cannot handle this city' to 'Man, cannot live away from this city' in just a couple of years.

I had bought a bike while I was in Lonavla. A Yamaha RXG, the next version of the hugely popular RX100 model. Once I became an officer, my weekend trips to Pune were on my bike, naturally. People who have travelled from Lonavla to Pune before 2000 will remember how bad the roads were during the rains and how dangerous it could get because of the heavy traffic en route. I used to zip at 100 to 120 kilometres per hour (that was the max it could go) keeping my guardian angels pretty busy throughout the drives. This happened every weekend.

However, in Vizag, I realised one thing the very first day I took my bike out. This was not a place for speed. I still remember, I was riding on the main road of the city. It was a wide road with decent traffic on it and I saw an elderly man riding a bike coming from a lane (not crossroads) on my left at full speed and continuing right across the road to another lane on the other side of the road with absolutely no reduction in speed. I had to brake and watch this phenomenon happening right in front of me. He never bothered to look left or right. Anyway, my speed immediately fell to the 30s in Vizag. I learned to be vigilant on these roads as these guerrilla drivers could pounce from the most unexpected corners.

My bike was a part of me. The first vehicle is always close to your heart, isn't it? I can see most guys nodding their heads vigorously. My bike was my buddy. I had even named it 'Gutsy' and had put up a sticker on the side of the seat. We used to go out everywhere together. Yeah, for me, going from place A to place B was Gutsy and I going together and yes, you would be right in thinking I did not have a girlfriend then. But that was not the reason I was attached to Gutsy.

Vizag, in 1998, was not at all a happening place. It was (and still is) an industrial city. You can make out the pulse of a city by the type of vehicles that are predominantly on the road. Take Mumbai, for example. It's a city comprised of professionals, businesspeople, entrepreneurs, and celebrities. So, you find mostly cars on the road. When you go to Pune, you find a perennially young crowd and mostly two-wheelers on the road because of all the educational institutions in the city. Similarly, Vizag being an industrial city, you mostly find trucks coming in from all parts of the country.

Our shipyard was located near the industrial area and there was a constant flow of trucks in and around the place.

There also weren't many interesting hangout places and there was nothing much to do after working hours in Vizag. Truth be told, it was boring, and I started to wonder how I would spend six whole months here. Munish was not the outgoing type (I guess he had a better vision for his life, compared to me, who was living one day at a time).

Then came the time for Navy week, which happens in December. This is the week of celebration in the Indian Navy. There are multiple activities organised by the Navy during this time. Ships are opened to visitors & school children, there could be a lunch feast for veterans, Naval band performances for the public and many more. The activities vary from one Naval command to another. The highlight of Navy week is Navy Day. It is celebrated every year to commemorate Operation Trident, which was the attack on the Karachi harbour during the Indo-Pakistan war (on 4 December 1971). The Saturday following Navy Day is the big event—Navy Ball. A couple of decades back, this was the only true-blue, high society, large event that happened even in a city like Mumbai. We did not have too many parties or pubs at that time and getting a ticket was a matter of pride and something that gave people a chance to show off. It truly is an amazing spectacle seeing all the officers in their sparkling uniforms (6Bs) along with their wives or girlfriends (some real and some 'managed') in their best party dresses, dancing and having a great time. The dances start with proper ballroom music where some, especially senior officers who are trained in ballroom dancing, take to the dance floor while others, the lesser mortals, stand around and clap. As the evening progresses, the music becomes peppier and dances become Bollywoodesque, giving us, the 'untrained' dancers a chance to get on the dance floor to move our booty and finally, as the food stalls get empty and the liquor in the liquor stand gets transferred to the persistent ones still going strong on the dance floor, the music gravitates towards Punjabi and the officers in their fine uniform and the ladies in their exquisite gowns resort to *bhangra*.

There are two types of young officers—the ones who have girlfriends and the ones who don't. Navy Ball is the time when the first category proudly struts their girlfriend around. These officers also come into a lot of demand during this time because the best way to have a 'girlfriend' during the ball (when you don't have a real one) is to request one of these real girlfriends to get their friends for a night of dance and music (and free drinks, of course). It saves them from looking like losers during the ball. There is also a Navy Queen contest, which used to be a sure entry to the Miss India contest or even Bollywood (especially for the Mumbai Navy queen). Well, nothing much happened for Munish and me during the Navy Ball that year at Vizag, and we ended up going as stags. But my life took a new turn in the next event of Navy week, which was the Navy Mela. This is a three-day event, and it is like an exhibition. There are many units and ships that would put up their stalls for various things. There are stalls where information on how to join the Indian Navy is shared and there are also other commercial stalls set up with plenty of food stalls in between. It is a great place to spend the evenings.

I decided to spend my evening at the Navy Mela and there, I met Payal. She was very chirpy, easy to talk to and was also from a defence background. So, we connected very easily. The bigger thing that happened was that through her, I met Raju, a dashing youngster who was already an entrepreneur running a fashion technology company. They were my first civilian friends in Vizag. Raju became the pillar or the cornerstone of everything that I achieved at a later stage in my life. His thoughts and ideas were way ahead of their time and unfortunately, his fashion technology institute did not do too well. Raju had an indomitable spirit that never gave up and he went on to build a business empire single-handedly that is worth thousands of crores today. Today, he flies around in his own aircraft, and it takes months to get to meet him, even if it is for a short duration.

However, back in 1998, he was a totally carefree person. Payal, Raju, and I became the best of friends. This friendship gave me the best times I had in Vizag. I started looking forward to 'All hands down' which meant the end of work for the day on board. I would quickly bathe and head out to meet them and we would spend the evenings together doing something fun.

None of us had a lot of money. So, it was all about spending time together, sitting by the beach and having conversations, Raju pulling some prank on us or planning a movie over the weekend, etc. He was (and still is) a foodie and knew the best places where the tastiest food was served. He once took me home where he lived with his mom and twin sisters. He made prawn curry and rice for me, and we all had a lot of fun sitting around and talking. He had lost his dad at an early age and his family was everything to him (and still is) and he would do everything in his might to make sure that they had a good life. The three of us became very close and we spent all evenings roaming around on our bikes, sometimes riding triples on Raju's Splendor bike. We played Holi with eggs (I know!). It was fun for us. The standard operating procedure was that one would ride the bike and the other would sit behind with a fresh egg in hand and he would break it on someone's head (mostly on Payal's because of her long(er) hair). Did you know that eggs make your hair silky smooth? Go ahead and try it once. After playing Holi, we would go to Gangawaram beach to wash up. Then we would go back, change clothes and head out again. Spending time together became a daily affair. I don't really remember any single time when we were not together, evenings on weekdays and full days on weekends.

Payal always wanted to join the Indian Armed Forces. She was the leader in her NCC squad of her college where she studied, and she took a lot of pride in it. We had the Republic Day parade on the beach road of Vizag and there were contingents from various ships and naval bases as well as from schools and other organisations. Naturally there was a contingent from NCC as well and Payal was leading the contingent. I remember calling her out and beckoning her to come to me. Since we both were in uniforms, she had no choice but to salute me in front of everyone. I did that a couple of times for my amusement and to watch her fume since she knew I was doing it deliberately.

Life became exciting for me even in a place like Vizag and I was very happy. I was loving my life professionally as well. I was learning a lot of things about marine engineering and watchkeeping. One of the early lessons that got imprinted literally (almost on my face) was about steam. My ship was a steamship, which means that the turbines that propelled the ship were driven with steam and the steam was generated in the boiler. The boiler room was massive with all kinds of pipes snaking all over the place. I had only seen normal steam until then. I had not seen (still can't see) superheated steam. And this was the lesson I learned—the difference between steam and superheated steam is that you can't *see* superheated steam. The ship was old, the pipes were old and there were many places where there was leakage of superheated steam. If you were not careful, you could get badly burned while inspecting the pipes or even while just passing between them. I also learned to deal with complex inter-departmental issues. It becomes even more complex when there is a chicken involved.

❋❋❋

When a ship sails, it takes on the ration required for its estimated period of sailing. It could be days, weeks or even months, though months are rare unless you are going on a cruise. The rations include all kinds of lentils, pulses, condiments, and everything else. It also has something called blast-frozen chicken. This is one step ahead of frozen chicken where the fresh chicken is frozen with a blast of cold air at minus 40 degrees to freeze the chicken instantly. This way, it gets frozen way below the normal frozen chicken temperature. This is done so that the chicken can remain fresh for months together.

All the frozen products are kept in a storage room called the 'Cold Room'. It's basically a walk-in freezer where all the meats and other eatables that need to be kept frozen are stored. All rations, including the ones in the cold room naturally come under the logistics department, which is responsible for all supplies, from salt to the engines of a ship and in this particular case, the chicken. Now, the cold room also comes under the engine room department as they are the ones maintaining the temperature of the cold room. During sailing, the ship follows a three-watch system (remember it?). The graveyard shift (watch in our case) which lasts all through the night is the time when the engine room staff gets naughty. They are supposed to take rounds of all machinery, including the cold room. I guess the inviting looks of a smiling chicken (all kinds of hallucinations happen late at night, right?) sometimes becomes too much. We could figure out these 'special' nights because the next morning, the logistics department would come to see one of the engine room officers with a complaint of a missing chicken that couldn't have decided to jump overboard at night. I used to wonder what they did with the blast-frozen chicken as the galley (kitchen in layman's terms) was locked at night and it also did not have any machinery inside for the engine room staff to go and check. What *can* someone do with a blast-frozen chicken (which is harder than frozen chicken) with no cooking facilities?

One of the nights, while I was doing the rounds, I went down to the engine room and I saw the place almost deserted, except for the watchkeeper keeping a sharp eye on the engine parameters. I stepped out of the watchkeeper's cabin and saw a small huddle near one of the steam pipes. I went there and was welcomed warmly by the group. They were quite open with the two of us who were doing watchkeeping as we were 'hands-on' with them when it came to repairs, et cetera. I learned a very important use of superheated steam that night. I'd never seen a frozen chicken cook that quickly in my life before. All you had to do was put the frozen chicken in a bowl and keep it under a steam dump. If you thought Maggi cooked in two minutes, this cooked even faster, and yes, they were kind enough to bring their own Maggi noodles to make it a proper meal.

❋❋❋

Another important milestone during watchkeeping, which had a large impact on my professional life was that I got introduced to this wonderful thing called computers. Today, even kindergarten kids are familiar with computers and other devices, but it was not the case for us in 1998. I had seen one desktop computer in school when I was in the 10th grade and a few in college, but I had never gotten the chance to sit down in front of one and operate those fascinating machines on my own. Even though I studied computer science as one of the subjects in my engineering, the most exciting thing for me was to sit in the AC room of the computer wing and see how the instructors operate these machines. Also, those were mostly DOS[18]-based and did not have Windows as Operating System. To my pleasant surprise, our engine room office had one all to ourselves. I was totally captivated by the amazing machine. It had the latest (then the latest) Windows 95 loaded as well. I used to spend a lot of time trying out different things on the computer. Unlike what I thought earlier, I learned that the metal part of a floppy was to protect the disc inside and not for us to hold it without damaging the plastic (yes, I was that ignorant about computers).

There was a software that was being used on board ships for diesel engines back then. It was called ADETA (Automated Diesel Engine Trend Analysis). It was a DOS-based system (means it did not have any colours. It was all typing commands and boring looks). Seeing my interest in computers, my Commander (E), Cdr Bahri, asked me to study the system and prepare a presentation on its advantages and disadvantages. I couldn't be happier. I did exactly that and showed it to him and he said the Commander-in-Chief wanted to know our findings. I was on top of the world. From not knowing how to hold a floppy a few weeks ago to making a presentation about a software to a flag officer (senior officers who are allowed to fly a flag on their cars indicating their rank), that too the Commander-in-Chief of the Eastern Naval Fleet. Naturally, I was nervous throughout the presentation and the Commander-in-Chief, of course, noticed it. But after the presentation ended, he asked what the solution was, and we astutely suggested that the software needed to be made in Windows as this was the future. The Chief agreed, nodded his head, thought for a moment, and said, 'Fine. Make it.'

---

[18]**Disk Operating System**, is an operating system that runs from a disk drive. The term can also refer to a particular family of disk operating systems, most commonly MS-DOS, an acronym for Microsoft DOS

Cdr Bahri had an M.Tech in computer science but naturally, the task was given to me. My excitement was akin to that of a headless chicken. I was running all around the place (in my head) excited, had absolutely no clue what to do, and I knew I could end up in the slaughterhouse if I couldn't make it. That did not stop me. Nothing could have stopped me from doing some actual work on a computer. I worked day and night on the project. Not philosophically, but actually. Both the night duty as well as the morning duty personnel used to see me crouched next to the computer, trying to figure things out. Little did I know then that God was prepping me for a drastic change in my life and career ahead. After a month or two, I was ready with the Windows version of the software, and I had to start installing it on board other ships and take feedback. It was a large program and required multiple floppy discs to copy and transport and I was the only person who knew how to install it (yes! This was a galaxy far, far away that did not have pen drives and CDs).

CHAPTER 6

THE DEATH BRIDGE AND THE DEMONS

Despite all these exciting things happening with computers and programs, the core duty for Munish and me was always Engine Room watchkeeping and it was also going great alongside. We were learning and enjoying a lot. One day, we realised that we had not started doing one of the most important aspects of watchkeeping—journal writing. Whatever we learned on board had to be translated into a thick journal which had to be submitted and checked prior to receiving the watchkeeping certificate. Although we had started writing, we had a lot of catching up to do in that area. We decided that we would be totally committed to that task from then on, and to display our commitment (mostly to ourselves), we decided to chuck all other work and dedicate our evenings after work to journal writing.

One evening, we decided to cut off all distractions and sit in the Operations Room and write the journal. I was totally in with the plan. Well, as long as I could go out on weekends, especially the coming one because Raju and Payal had made plans with me to go for a picnic at a beach where we were to cook meals and devour them. My role was mostly as the cheerleader and morale booster as culinary skills were restricted to Payal and Raju. That picnic was to be followed up with the movie *Titanic* and Raju was to book tickets. We took our journals and sat down in the Ops room as planned. It was a Friday and the ship's company had retired for the weekend except for the duty personnel. The married ones went home, and the bachelors stayed on board.

One of the senior bachelors on board, Lt Cdr Seth had just got posted out—that too, to a prestigious post—and all the live-in officers were celebrating in the wardroom (the dining and recreational area for officers). Munish and I had decided that we would not be part of it as we had a lot of work to catch up on. While writing the journal, Munish felt thirsty and went to the wardroom[19] to have water. When he came back, he said that every single live-in officer was there celebrating, and we were the only ones left out. I also felt that it was not fair that we were not there celebrating his posting since Seth sir had helped us a lot during our stay on board. We decided to just pop in and congratulate him and then promptly come back to the Ops room and continue with our task of writing the journal. To ensure that we would come back, we left the journals open. Unfortunately, I never got a chance to close mine.

※ ※ ※

---

[19] Wardroom is the place where officers have meals and is also used for recreation

I hear screams.

I hear people shout at the top of their voices.

I don't feel anything.

Someone tries to pick me up.

I feel a hand around my shoulder.

I can't see anything properly.

I can't hear anything clearly.

I am semiconscious.

I try to focus my eyes.

I see bright lights of vehicles.

I see people running in front of the lights.

I look down at my leg.

I see a pool of blood.

I lose consciousness.

I hear the loud sound of an autorickshaw engine.

I feel hands hold my stretched out body tight.

I hear someone shout 'Drive fast, buddy. Drive fast!'

I lose consciousness.

I hear someone shout 'Emergency, emergency, get the stretcher immediately.'

Someone lifts me onto a stretcher.

I hear the wheels of the stretcher moving very fast.

I see lights on the roof pass me quickly.

I feel my body shaking on the stretcher.

I lose consciousness.

I see a bright, round light right on top of me.

I hear a familiar voice, 'Bimal, you will be fine.'

I see someone with a large pair of scissors.

I feel my jeans being torn apart.

I lose consciousness.

I hear the gentle beeps of monitors.

I hear muffled voices. I see a nice cubicle.

I see two people in white coats over their uniforms standing next to me.

I see an elderly nurse in her white uniform at the end of my bed.

I see she has a kind face.

I see her gently nod in quiet assurance.

I lose consciousness.

When I got back to my senses, I was in the ICU of INS Sanjivani, the Naval Hospital in Vizag. I tried to recount the events after we left the Ops room to wish Lt Cdr Seth in the wardroom.

❖❖❖

We had gone there to congratulate Seth sir and sat down with them for a while. Everyone was happy and celebrating with music and drinks. A table was booked at Hotel Horizon, which was one of the nicest hotels with live music in Vizag at the time. Everyone was to leave for dinner there. Munish and I looked at each other. 'Everyone is going for dinner together. We are the only ones missing from the in-living lot. Let us keep this as our last outing. We can work a little bit longer after we come back from dinner.'

That was the final decision. It really wasn't fair that we did not participate in such a big occasion.

So, we let our 'hair down' (I know, we hardly had any). Everyone was drinking but I was a teetotaller back then. Therefore, I decided to teach them the steps of the dance *Macarena*, which was hugely popular at the time. I still love the song, but it was quite fresh those days. We clicked photographs after which we decided to leave for dinner. We had about five or six bikes to accommodate all of us. I was on Gutsy and my assistant engineer, Lieutenant Harish, decided to ride with me. How he came to be on my bike was also interesting.

He had his own sports bike. It was a hotshot bike with more power than its contemporaries and boy, did it sound deadly! He, unfortunately, also had a history of accidents. Some people used to joke about him that he was someone who had to meet with at least one minor accident every year. We used to hear about him falling off the bike, et cetera, in Shivaji as well, when we were cadets, and he was an officer.

Unfortunately, I came to know all these things only much later. If I had known it that night, perhaps I would've asked him to ride with someone else. He did take his bike out that night as well, but he realised that he was quite drunk, and may not be safe for him to ride it. He called one of the youngsters, who was a midshipman (yes, we had this rank those days). He gave him the keys to his sports bike, and the youngster was like a kid who got the latest toy. He started the bike and went boom-boom with the accelerator. Seeing that, Harish sir felt that he may not be the safest driver. He looked around and saw me. He instinctively knew that I was the safest among all, he told me. After all, I was a reformed speedster.

All of us went out of the dockyard with my bike leading the pack. Just outside the dockyard was an infamous, narrow bridge. It was more like a death bridge. Every single year, at least one naval personnel would die on that bridge or the road leading to it. A lot of things were done to prevent it. Speed breakers were added before and after the bridge, there were warning signs put up everywhere, but the deaths continued to happen. It was very spooky. And like I mentioned earlier, Vizag was an industrial city and the most common vehicle that we could see on roads those days were trucks coming from all over the country and they plied on the roads next to the dockyard as well, as some of the sulphur factories were situated nearby.

That night, I was coming out of the narrow bridge and there was a truck coming into the bridge from the other side. It seems (I came to know about all this much later after the accident) that there was a dog that came in front of the truck. Maybe the truck driver was caught unaware, maybe he was scared of the animal rights' people, but whatever the reason, he swerved to avoid the dog and lost control and I had a head-on collision with the truck. I don't even remember all these details because I think my mind has blocked them out. Anyway, I hit my right shin (the part of the leg below the knee) on the bumper of the truck, and it broke into pieces (my shin, that is). The impact was so bad that I got thrown off my bike and hit the face of the truck headfirst. One side of my helmet got crushed. Then I went up in the air and landed on the road, again headfirst, crushing the other side of the helmet as well.

Later, people who saw my helmet refused to believe that the person who was wearing it was alive. I did not have even a scratch on my head, thanks to my helmet.

There is a concept called connecting the dots and even though I didn't know about all this, when I look back, I realize that I had bought my helmet only for this incident. After I bought Gutsy, I went helmet hunting. Those days (in 1997), you could get a really good helmet for about 600 to 700 Indian rupees. For some reason, I never liked any of them.

When I was in Pune, I went with Harish to a sports shop, and I saw a massive helmet kept there. I tried it on, and I felt very, very safe (yes, I actually did). I still remember that moment. It was a special helmet, the kind used by racers which covered most of your face and was made with a special Kevlar mix and all (I wonder why I still remember all these details even now). No one even used to even borrow my helmet because it was so huge. Well, that big, huge helmet saved my life. I always tell people not to penny-pinch when buying a helmet. It technically is for single use. And when it gets used, it might just decide whether you live or die.

Back in the ICU, I was put on 'the list'. At the hospital, there are two lists when it comes to injuries and diseases—DIL and SIL. Nothing romantic about it. It means Dangerously Ill List and Seriously Ill List. DIL means the person is about to die, the NOK (Next of Kin) is informed, and flight tickets are sent to them to fly in and visit the ward maybe for one last time. SIL is one step lower, and the NOK does not get flight tickets 😌

In the ICU, I lived my life from moment to moment. I was given a lot of sedatives and painkillers. Days and nights ceased to exist for me. It was just the time when I was awake or deep in sleep. Every day, a medical assistant came and added one more layer to the full-length cast that started right below my hip and extended all the way to my toes. It was strange because I had never seen a red-coloured cast. Only later did I realize that the cast was indeed white, but they could not stop the constant bleeding because of the injuries. I don't really remember pain during my stay in the ICU. I had many senior officers visiting me, known and unknown to me. I am sure the accident would have been the major point of discussion in the dockyard at least for a couple of days until something more interesting came up.

The constant presence I remember was of Payal and Raju. They bunked college, and let the institute be run by someone else, but they were there every single time I opened my eyes, except at night-time when no one is allowed in the ICU. Payal would be next to me, and Raju would be outside. It was like having my parents or my sisters around me. Only they would have the natural urge to be next to me. Not as a duty but as the most natural thing to do. Seeing them every time I opened my eyes was the most emotionally healing medicine I had. I still remember their concerned faces in front of me and my heart still swells up. One day, Payal wanted to feed me grapes and after taking permission from the duty nurse, she started feeding me one by one and as luck would have it, the skin of one of the grapes got stuck in my throat. It would have been a funny scene in a movie but I started coughing and with every cough, I used to cry out in pain. Payal just didn't know what to do. She ran and called the nurse and started crying.

Now, when we talk about this incident, we laugh.

The biggest challenge for the doctors was the catch-22 situation I was in. Vizag did not have orthopaedic facilities required to treat me. I had to be airlifted to either Kolkata or Mumbai which had the command hospitals. To save my life, I had to be shifted to the

Command Hospital, but my condition was so bad that they could not afford to move me anywhere. I was kept under strict observation to see if my condition was stabilizing so that they could take a call on moving me. Finally, after more than 10 days of uncertainty, they decided to airlift me to Kolkata.

Raju was there until the chopper took off with me taking me to the commercial airport. Unfortunately, I was under deep sedation for the journey ahead and I have no recollection of the entire event. I remember opening my eyes and finding myself on a stretcher on the floor of an aircraft. Seeing my eyes open, one of the very good-looking hostesses, who, out of their training to serve others, kneeled next to me and asked me politely, 'Sir, are you in any kind of discomfort?'

I wanted to laugh but I could only manage a smile and I guess she understood. She quickly apologised and left me to go back into a deep sleep.

Command Hospital Kolkata (it was Calcutta then) is a super-speciality hospital where some of the best military surgeons are posted. In those days, it was a very crucial treatment facility as it was the hub for the entire north eastern sector of India. There were a lot of ULFA[20] activities happening in those days in the northeastern states and the years preceding them. The activities had just started dwindling around the time I was there. For all the casualties of the northeast, this super speciality hospital was the singular destination.

My operation was scheduled for the following morning. I remember waking up in terrible pain as someone was cutting through my cast. They had to use a manual cutter, which was

---
[20]ULFA - The United Liberation Front of Asom is an armed separatist organisation operating in the Northeast Indian state of Assam. It seeks to establish an independent sovereign nation state of Assam for the indigenous Assamese people through an armed struggle in the Assam conflict.

basically like a pair of large scissors attached to the end of a long rod. I still don't know why they didn't use an electric saw like they used every other time the plaster had to be changed. Maybe my cast was too soggy because of the blood all over it, or maybe they did not have an electric point in the prep room (which was unlikely). I knew the name of the Colonel who was to do my surgery and I was assured that he was one of the best in the country. But for me, he was THE best because he was able to put all my bones together. My shin (tibia & fibula - for the doctors reading this and squirming at the use of layman's words) had shattered and looked more like a bouquet than bones. My kneecap (patella) went missing and was assumed to have been crushed in the accident. Surgeon Colonel Sinha was not only able to give a proper shape to my leg by putting all the broken pieces together, but he also found my kneecap on the opposite side of where it was supposed to be and put it back where it belonged. When I think of it now, it was indeed a miracle that it did not get crushed in the accident.

I woke up the next morning with seven rods hammered into my shin to keep the bones in place. There was also one smaller rod that went right through and across my shin, just below my kneecap. Two strings were attached on either side of this smaller rod, which went straight to the far end of the bed and over two small pulleys and were attached to some weights. The lower end of the bed was propped up on a block. This was basically to prevent bleeding by reducing the blood flow to my leg. The weights were used to pull my thigh bone (femur) away from my hip (acetabulum). Yes, I had a fractured and dislocated hip as well. It was my right side that took the brunt since I hit the truck at an angle. My body above my hip as well as my entire left side was miraculously intact. Looking back, it was such a blessing not to have any head injury in such a big accident and to have an entire side intact.

Now that I was in proper ortho care after the major operation, I was not under heavy sedation during the day. I was given a sedative and painkiller injection only at night to help me sleep. My bones were held together with external fixators (the seven rods hammered into my bone) and my hip was pulled down with the rope and pulley. The only movement I could do was to lift my torso using a handle that dangled over the bed, like the ones we see in Mumbai locals (yes, it is true that hospital beds at that time did not always have levers and fancy buttons that would gently prop you up or take you down as and when required). No sedation also meant that my senses were back and therefore, the pain.

When my parents were initially informed about the accident, they were also in a catch-22 situation. It had an extra angle to it. First of all, they didn't know whether to come to Vizag or the city I was to be transferred to because my condition was fluctuating. There was no point in landing in Vizag only to learn that I have been transferred. So, they had to wait and decide. Added to this, *Achan* had had a heart attack just a few months prior to my accident and he was under strict restrictions, travel included. I guess for any parent, risks for their own health are far less important when it comes to their children's well-being. They met his doctor out of courtesy just to inform him that they were travelling out to meet me, and the doctor gave them the required advice regarding precautions.

My parents had never really left Kerala ever. The only travel my father undertook was to take my elder sister for an interview in Chennai. They never spoke Hindi or English even though they knew both languages. It is a common factor among *Malayalis* that our written Hindi and English are far better than spoken because we never converse in those languages. The biggest help that we got was from our cousin Dr Sherly (Preethi *Chechi* to me), my mom's sister's daughter, and her husband, Dr Unnikrishnan or *Unniyettan*[21] as we lovingly call him. For me, they are more than family. I am indebted to them for life, not only for this, but for many more things. For me, right from my school and college days, my vacations were never complete until I went and spent some days, sometimes weeks, with them (their kids were my favourite nieces, Parvathy and Lakshmi). Preethichechi was and will always be like a mother to me. Even though it was board exam time for their elder daughter, Parvathy, Unniyettan decided to accompany my parents. The fact that they are both excellent doctors themselves gave more confidence to my parents. You see, he was someone who could read case sheets and make out what exactly was happening.

Meanwhile, something else was happening to my sister, Minichechi, who was based in Delhi at the time. When my parents came to know that I was shifted to Kolkata, naturally the onus fell on Minichechi to figure out how to reach out to me or the hospital.

The day after I reached the Command Hospital, she found out the board number and called the hospital. After multiple tries, she got connected to the right place but at the wrong time. When she got connected, I was in the post-operative ward, screaming in pain as the anaesthesia was wearing out. I had mentioned in the beginning about my sisters that they are more like mothers to me. Yeah, I have four mothers that way, including Preethichechi. Once she heard my screams, she broke down. She decided she had to meet me somehow and applied for leave. So, she was also on her way to meet me.

The initial days at the hospital were nice for me because my parents and Unniyettan came and spent time with me, and they

---

[21] Ettan in Malayalam language means elder brother. It can also be someone elder who is referred endearingly as ettan. Many wives call their husbands Ettan.

were there everyday until the end of visiting hours at 2000h. In about a month, Unniyettan had to go back. My parents stayed back and after a few more weeks, my father also had to go back to take care of his health. *Amma* stayed back alone.

I think nothing can come close to a mother's willpower and tenacity when it comes to her children. *Amma* stayed back all alone in a city where she knew no one and didn't even know the language. I am indebted to my commanding officer, Commodore PP Singh of INS Vindhyagiri. When he came to know that my parents were coming to Kolkata, he arranged for their stay in the Naval mess at INS Netaji Subhash which was about 5 km away from the hospital. He even made sure that there was a vehicle to pick them up and drop them to the hospital every single day. I never did get the chance to meet him and thank him for all that he did for my parents. Once my mother extended her stay, they could not always provide a means of transport for her. She would come out and take an auto rickshaw or a taxi to come to the hospital. I remember *Amma* learning a little bit of Hindi from me. What do you say for left, what do you say for right, to stop, and the like. Those days are special to me because I got to know her a little better.

I asked her about her growing-up years and she shared stories of how they used to walk to school, even during rains, how they went swimming in the river near their home and how their home was, her parents, sisters, everything. I had never heard these stories from her until then. I realize that even though we do spend a lot of time with our parents, we know very little about their lives prior to our birth, especially their childhood. She shared the love story of one of her sisters and how my uncle would write poems for my aunt, describing her beauty. It was delightful listening to her.

Amma would be there by my side by 0800h every day like clockwork and we would spend the entire day together till she had to leave by about 2000h. She would talk to me about her life, sometimes read to me and a couple of times, even sing to me when I insisted. She would hold my hand while I screamed when the nursing assistants dressed my wound every day. In the afternoon, she would sit next to my bed on a chair and put her head on the bed and sleep for a while and I would read something that time.

There was another uncle, who is a relative of *Amma* who lived in Kolkatta. Sukumaran uncle was a short, soft-spoken gentleman who used to come and visit me once a week and get me some delicious homemade *mallu* food. I used to look forward to his visits every week.

While *Amma* was there, Minichechi also landed at the hospital with her two kids. She brought along with her a Walkman which had a small speaker so that I could listen to music and a book by James Herriot, *All Creatures Great and Small*. I fell in love with the book and later went on to read all of his books. It was like a family get-together at the hospital with *Amma*, Minichechi and my nephews. They used to sit around and talk to me and share interesting stories. My sister went back after about a week to 10 days and my mother went back after about three months. Once my honeymoon period in the hospital was over and everyone left, *they* came for me.

My demons.

Even while my family was there with me, passing each day was a difficult task. I was a workaholic. I not only used to work whole nights on my software project (ADETA), but I also happily worked with machinery on board when there was any kind of issues. One of the features of INS Vindhyagiri was its guns. It had two massive 330 mm guns which made it the gun ship for operations. The pressure required to fire the guns came from two HP (High Pressure) air pumps. I remember that once, we needed the guns but the pump had conked off. Such big guns are of no use if they can't fire, right? It was a huge task of getting the HP air pumps going and I used to work with the staff entire nights during sailing to get them back online. And all this was happening just before the accident. For me, being confined to a bed was like making a racing sports car apply sudden brakes out of the blue. The inactivity of just lying on the bed, looking at the ceiling, was killing me. My only escape was the conversations I used to have with my mother and sister (while they were there)

It is said that ignorance is bliss, and it was true for me initially. I never had any hospitalisation prior to this and no one in my family had any fractures of any kind. I had heard that when you get a fracture, you need to have a cast for four to six weeks maximum. I took that as my baseline and being the enthu cutlet that I was, I started planning my career once the eight weeks were done (gave my surgeon two extra weeks since my 'fracture' looked a little complex with rods and stuff). I used to ask the doctor as to when I would get discharged. I mean, if I knew the date, my planning could be even better, right? He used to just smile and tell me not to worry about discharge dates and all. I had mentioned that I was doing MESC (Marine Engineering Specialisation Course) and the only course which was on board a ship was the Engine Room Watchkeeping. Therefore, my plan was pretty logical (according to me). My medical restriction, once I get discharged, would be about going back to a ship, that too for a year or so till I am fully healed. I could always complete the rest of the courses (which were part of specialisation) and then go back for watchkeeping at the end of it by which time I would be fully recovered and healed. Brilliant plan, isn't it?

• • •

The only challenge was that it wasn't a plan, it was more of wishful thinking as the reality was very different. Even though the initial operation was successful, and the surgeon was able to find all the bones that were available and put them together, they really did not know if I would be able to walk normally again. Of course, they never told me all this at the time.

As days turned into weeks, hope began to wane. The pain I was going through did not help either. I was on the top floor of the hospital and there was a grill-less window next to my bed. When I looked out of the window while lying down on my bed, I could only see the top of a few nearby buildings. Days were okay since I was on painkiller tablets throughout the day, but I dreaded the nights. Every night, after dinner, I was given a painkiller-sedative injection for the night. I used to fall asleep easily but in about six hours, the effects of the medicine would start wearing off and I would wake up in excruciating pain. I had a bell right next to me for emergencies, but no one used to come because they knew what was happening and they could not do anything for me at that time. This combination of excruciating pain coupled with the effect of medicines wearing off was the worst. In that daze, I used to hallucinate.

When I looked out of the same window, instead of rooftops, I could see a very ugly-looking mountain and people chasing me with knives with a clear intention to kill me. I remember screaming, asking for help. I just could not go back to sleep. I saw every single sunrise for the first couple of months that I was there, even while my mother was there. When she was there, I used to wait for her to come in the morning to take my mind away from all the ghastly thoughts that I was having. I even used to complain to her about all that I was seeing at night. All she could do was comfort me and assure me that everything was going to be fine.

❦❦❦

Comforting is always an easy task when you don't have to go through what the other person is going through. At a logical level, I knew that my fears at night were misplaced, and I could reassure myself by looking out of the same window to see the same old rooftops. However, at night, I would get transported to this evil place where I would be attacked and hunted by people and demons. I even asked the nurse once why no one bothered to come when I rang the emergency bell that was next to me. She said very sweetly that they all understood what I was going through, but they could not do anything about it as the next set of painkillers could be given only after breakfast. It wasn't that they did not care, they were clinically detached from the pain and suffering that I was going through. I made sure that I did not sleep during the day because that would also make me wake up at nights. But nothing helped me.

The demons of the nights started crawling up on my bed during the day as well. This time they were not hallucinations but logical reasoning about my life, my career, my future. I realised slowly that even the doctors were kind of hoping that I would be able to walk properly again. Every day, medical assistants used to come to clean and dress the wound. I could not really call it a wound because most of the flesh on my calf had been ripped off. That was the reason I was on external fixators and not on a full-length cast, as it is normally done for fractures.

The realisation started creeping up on me slowly that I was going to be stuck here for a long, long time. I knew about some other officers who had been there for many months for various reasons. I could literally see the ugly faces of my demons blowing off the positive spirit that I was desperately trying to hold on to. I could see and almost hear their evil laugh and I started getting a sinking feeling. A pit in the stomach, a heaviness in the heart and a numbness in my spirit. It was a really bad combination to have for anyone struggling to come out of a low phase in life.

My career, my life, my health, my future. Everything suddenly looked very bleak to me. My ugly-looking leg reminded me that it may never get fully healed, told me about the scar that I was going to have even if it got better, that I will never walk properly (forget running) ever again, that my dreams of joining the submarine arm, where a lot of my coursemates were, was just that… an impossible dream. It even shared with me, with logical conviction, that no girl in her right mind would want to be with someone who has such disfigurement and disability at such a young age.

Being totally bedridden has another very painful aspect to it. The bedpan. One of the most helpless feelings that anyone can get is when the most private moments of your life get dependent on other people and their convenience. I could not even wipe myself and I just had to lie there while someone else did it for me. Some people may call it losing my dignity. For me, it was far from dignity. It was sheer helplessness I felt every time I had to 'go to the toilet' as they say.

Most days, my body clock had a general timing like early morning and maybe late in the evening when it was just the hospital staff. I remember a couple of times when my clock decided to take a break. I had to go right during visiting hours, and I could not hold off any longer. The assistants didn't care if there were people around. For them, my comfort was paramount, and they just put a temporary screen around my bed and gave me the bedpan. My room had four beds which were occupied and there were visitors right next to my bed. I still remember seeing through the gaps of the temporary screen, the disgusted looks on the faces of people as they covered their noses with whatever they could find.

I still get emotional when I think of this moment. I don't think I have ever felt that helpless in my life. As tears rolled down my face, I asked God why he didn't just finish me in the accident rather than making me go through such humiliation. As a coach today, I would have counselled my younger self from having such negative thoughts. However, at that point of time, I did not have the wisdom that I have today. It was just me all alone fighting my demons, being helpless and having to use the dreaded pan. I was the one going through and living the experience and I had every right to feel what I felt at the time. Some nurses understood what I was going through, and they would come to me later and just hold my hand, telling me it was alright. I wanted to just get up, hug them and cry.

There was one more time when I was really pissed with God for not ending my life. One night, as I was fighting my demons, for some weird reason, I needed the bedpan. I tried a lot to hold off, but I could not. I started calling out to the nurses and pressed the bell repeatedly, desperately wanting someone to come to my bed. Unfortunately, they were used to my screams and bellringing by then and they chose to ignore all my pleas and cries. I ended up lying on the bed all through the night to early morning with my waste as my companion.

I stopped shouting for help. I just lay there, not even in a position to move my body since threads and pulleys and weights were attached to me making sure that I didn't move much. I was beyond feeling helpless. I had become numb and stopped reacting. Through my tears, I just told God that I hated him. This had to be deliberate. I had suffered enough. I was suffering daily, and I didn't need more at that point in life.

I was told initially by one of the nurses that when the fractured hip starts healing, it could be a painful affair and one night, it happened. Despite all the medications and painkillers, my hip was hurting like crazy, and I just could not sleep. The duty nurse was very sweet and caring. She sat next to me the whole night keeping hot water bags under my hip, trying to ease the pain. I wish I had the technology that we have today. I could have had pictures with them, would have been able to be in touch with them, be able to help them out if I could. Other than the sweet memories and a heart full of gratitude, I have nothing else with me today for all the nurses and assistants who cared for me, cheered me on, and held my hand when I broke down. I just can't thank them enough in this lifetime or the next.

The more I thought about the accident, the more it did not make any sense to me. Of all the people in that entire group, I was the only one who wasn't drunk that fateful night. The assistant engineer (Lt Harish) who was with me on my bike sustained only minor injuries. What did I do so wrong in my life that I had to bear the full brunt for it? I consider myself a good man. I was even nicer then than I am now. I never meant harm to anyone, never cheated anyone and always believed in the goodness of people and the world in general. I just could not get my head around it.

The challenge with people who have worked in the IT sector is that their thinking becomes very logical and sequential. There must be logic to everything. That is how software programs are written. The loops must close. The program must execute without bugs. There cannot be anything unknown in the program. Even though I was not in the IT sector at that time, I was someone who was driven by logic. Everything that I experienced had to have some logic to it and in this case, I just could not find any at all.

I knew that this whole episode was a grave mistake that must have happened at the highest level (God must have said, 'Oops!') and I started having major conversations with him. I was angry, I was frustrated, I felt helpless and more than anything else, I felt betrayed. I have seen people getting away after doing bad things, really bad things and nothing happening to them. I had even challenged the unofficial concept that was there during my cadet days (remember the *do-anything-but-don't-get-caught* philosophy?). I had asked the CO of INS Shivaji as to why this was encouraged because I believed that it is more important to have a solid value system and operate from that instead of trying shortcuts and smart acts and trying to get away with wrongdoings.

If I believed and operated out of the goodness of my heart as well as others, this should not be happening to me. I was sure that I had never intentionally harmed anyone in my life. There was no logical reason for my suffering, my pain, and my betrayal. The more I thought about it, the more I got upset. The more I argued with God, the angrier I became. This went on, on a daily basis, and I was turning into a sad, depressed, angry and constantly upset person who did not like to talk to anyone, smile or even sympathize with someone else. I started becoming the opposite of who I was before the accident. I was sad most of the time, snappy at people and was a very unhappy man, and I didn't like myself anymore.

Life became miserable for me. I stopped talking to people. I was constantly in a cycle of blaming God for everything, believing that what was happening to me was not fair and I should not be here, and I should not be suffering like this. I had reached a point where I could not handle it anymore. Dark thoughts started overwhelming me, my future looked bleak, and I was upset that all my coursemates were progressing in their careers while I was stuck in a hospital bed with no future.

One morning, as I started to ruminate on all the wrongs that were happening to me and how bad this God person was to make me suffer like this, especially since I was the only person in the entire gang (who went out for dinner) who was not drunk and so on, I had an epiphany. I remembered that I was in a similar situation (though not as grave) after my relegation.

When I analysed the sequence of events after that painful relegation, I realised that it was one of the best things to have ever happened to me. Since I was repeating the year and therefore all the classes, my grades had become much better. I came out of the shell that I had gone into for a few years prior to that. When I was in school, I was everything to the school. I was the drum major for the 40-piece school band that we were all proud of, I was the school leader and part of various initiatives. I was basically at the forefront of everything.

Somehow, when I came into the Navy, I saw too many people who were more than happy to jump at the opportunity to shine, take charge, and all that. I was never someone who took initiative just because I needed to prove something to others or even myself. I always had a quiet confidence in myself. Just that it became so quiet that only I seem to know about it.

After relegation, I became the 'senior most' in my division and my new coursemates, who had now become great friends, started to look up to me to step in and help in inter-divisional competitions like drama, dance, orchestra, et al, and I took it on without batting my eyelid. Earlier I was more of a team player as there were others leading it but now, I was leading everything. I directed a play, played the lead role, choreographed a multi-cultural dance sequence by teaching the steps to others and naturally, I was the lead singer in our band as well. One of my seniors who had graduated to become an officer remarked after watching one of the dramatics events that I choreographed, '*Where was this guy all these years?*'

Sitting on my bed in the hospital, sipping my tea, I no longer could just ignore or deny how my life had changed for the better after that relegation incident. Did I still see it as one of the worst things that happened to me? Did I still have all those emotions that I had when I went through it? The answer was staring right at my face. I was just not willing to look at the facts and take responsibility for my life. It was easier and maybe even comforting to blame everyone else for what happened. If it was not my fault, then it is not my responsibility to make things all right. God was bad to me. So, it's his responsibility to make this go away magically (He is supposed to be good at these things, right?).

I love peace and happiness. I think it is one of the basic human traits, to find happiness irrespective of the mess that they are in. They just need to get out of the blame game and 'poor-me' mode to find happiness and peace. All these thoughts helped me because I was forced to look at my situation very objectively and ask myself some hard questions. I had gotten fed up with my whining and constant complaining. I had enough and more reasons to continue to be in that state, but I realised that it was now up to me. I had to choose between being a victim or a warrior. I didn't feel like a warrior at that time, so I was fine with being a survivor. Anything better than a victim was a great start. I knew that the only way to move forward is to ask myself the question, 'What Next?'

Just the thought of asking myself that question was motivating for me because it was a clear indication that I was ready to move forward. However, to arrive at the stage where I could ask that question, I had to do some introspection. Ask myself some hard questions and be brutally honest with myself. You can lie to the whole world, but you really cannot lie to yourself, can you?

❋ ❋ ❋

The first step I had to do was separate fact from fiction or a story as I like to call it. What were the stories that I was making up?

- I should not be here, suffering.
- God betrayed me.
- It is totally unfair that I had the accident, and nothing happened to anyone else (misery loves company).
- My career is finished.
- I hate this hospital and all the people here.
- No one cares for me. Everyone has happily got on with their lives.
- My life is finished.

So on and so forth.

I had to write down the hard facts against each one of these.

- I should not be here, suffering. → Well, I am here and there is nothing I can do about it. As they say, pain is inevitable, but suffering is optional.
- God betrayed me → I don't even know his plans for me. Remember how things turned around after I lost a year. What do I know what plans he has for me after this?

- It is totally unfair that I had the accident, and nothing happened to anyone else → Why would I want anyone else to go through all that I went through? What does it speak about me as a friend and human being?
- My career is finished. → I have no real inputs to come to that conclusion. I could always complete my watchkeeping later and finish my courses after I gain back the strength to do so.
- I hate this hospital and all the people here. → This is one of the best orthopaedic facilities available in the country with one of the best surgeons in the country. I have experienced the love and care of all the nurses and caretakers. I have also not interacted with other people to decide whether to love or hate them.
- No one cares for me. Everyone has happily got on with their lives. → Definitely not a fact. Everyone I knew had come to meet me at the hospital. They happily gave their blood to me. I had received about 14 bottles of blood from others who wanted to help. They did everything that I would do for a friend or a coursemate. Raju and Payal were with me every single day at Vizag. Do I want them to go through all this?
- My life is finished. → Said the same last time as well but life turned out to be better because of the incident.

OMG! I said to myself as clarity dawned on me. It was scary because this was unfamiliar territory. I have never been in any accident in my life or hospitalised for any serious injuries like this. It was scary because I could no longer play the victim card. However, I was also excited because I was ready to ask the life-changing question. *What Next?*

CHAPTER 7

FIND YOUR FEET (FIGURATIVELY, OF COURSE!)

One of the most important steps when I ask the question 'What Next?' is to have a clear distinction between what was in my control and what wasn't. At the time, what was clearly not in my control was predicting how long my stay in the hospital would be. But what was in my control was how I could spend each day at the hospital, and I decided to focus on that.

One of the first things I put aside was my plans for the future. It is great to have a plan. However, If I had to accomplish something like completing my courses, I needed to have a start date or a reference date as to when I could start. Any plan without a reference or starting point was a sure way to invite more frustrations and disappointments into my life. I told myself that I would relook at my future only once my present was certain and clear. As a progression of this newfound perspective, my next task was to focus on each day as it came. One of my daily goals was to consciously be happy. It may seem silly, but it is a worthwhile goal for anyone to have on any given day of their lives.

Even though this is applicable and effective on all days, it is even more important when you are going through a difficult phase, especially something like a sickness. I didn't know any better that time, but now I see that even numerous researchers seem to agree with my thought process, which for me, was born out of a desperate need to not feel so horrible all through the day. If you google the importance of a positive mental attitude and happiness to personal health, you will get millions of articles and various methods on how you can remain happy and positive. Unfortunately, I did not have internet, social media, smartphones, or even basic phones (just this one line should be enough to push the latest iGen kids towards clinical depression).

Initially, looking at the mental state I was in, creating happiness was like making fire during the Stone Age. It was an arduous task with the limited resources available to me at a military hospital, till I had the realization that it was simply a matter of choice. I could just choose to be happy. It didn't require anything external.

We have no idea how much we take everything for granted. Do you remember how I was awake through the nights and how I had seen every single sunrise for almost three months? One night the duty nurse came to me and gave me the tablets at night and I dozed off, thanks to the painkillers. When I opened my eyes, I could see daylight. I had slept through the night. I did not wake up in pain in the middle of the night like I did until the previous night. I really did sleep all night.

I just could not believe it. I was like a child with a toy that he's been wanting all his life. It was like winning the lottery. I remember sharing my excitement with every single person who came anywhere near my bed. I told them with a 70mm smile, 'You know, I slept through the night!'

All of them except the nurses gave me confused looks. They were like, 'Dude, what is so exciting about sleeping through the night?' They just didn't get it.

I just thanked God that day for my gift of being able to sleep through the night, even if it was only one night. It is said that you realize the value of your eyesight only when you lose it. The same can be said about your sleep as well.

There is a huge load and weight that gets removed from your shoulders when you are not operating under the burden of future expectations. Most of the stress and grief in life happens because we either live in the past or we fear an uncertain future. The simple fact of the matter is this: the only thing we have is today, right now. If we can just start focusing on how we can live that to the best of our abilities, our future also gets taken care of.

There is nothing wrong in planning for the future or having goals. It is very important. I did not have a goal since I could not put a date to it, but my desire was to complete my Marine Engineering Specialisation. I had realised one important thing during my watchkeeping. Even though I wasn't the brightest in the course, I loved working with the engines, and I loved sailing. I loved marine engineering.

My first question, indeed, the most important one, was figuring out how I could spend each day in an interesting manner since I was bedridden. My movement was restricted to just lifting my upper body to rest my back while I propped myself up on the bed. I realised that I had been so caught up in my 'poor me' thoughts, I had forgotten about my love for reading.

There was an old lady with a kind face and sweet smile who used to come to the wards with a small cart full of books every day.

She was from the Red Cross, and she used to bring books to people who liked to read. I had ignored her completely as she was also one of those who betrayed me (What? Why? How? Doesn't matter because those who are in victim mode are adept at finding faults with everyone around them).

Smiling at her for a change did a lot of good as I realised that she did not hold any grudge towards me for having ignored her all those days. Maybe she does see a lot of people like me around. She was more than willing to lend me books that I could read throughout the day. I got so attached to reading that I started taking two books a day till one day she spoke to me in an apologetic tone, 'Sir, could you please read the books slowly? We don't have that many books in the library.' We both laughed but I also realised that I needed to find other ways of spending my time.

The second thing I took up was writing. I liked writing, not as an active practice, but whenever I used to be overwhelmed with emotions, I used to write my thoughts in the form of a story or a poem. Since I had many interesting events and incidents in my life, I decided to write about those. I had just finished a book by PG Wodehouse and I loved his writing style. I took on the same style and found myself smiling whenever I wrote. Humour is all about seeing the same things that we see every day but with a different eye. Writing became therapeutic for me.

One of the incidents that I wrote about was happening to me daily. On the bed next to mine was a veteran. I don't remember what he was admitted for, I think it was kidney stones, but I do remember that he suffered from constipation along with his other real issue. And how do I remember that you ask? Well, he decided to share his pain and entertain me with his ruminations on how his morning visit to the bathroom went every single day. Unfortunately, that happened to be the same time when my breakfast was served with sunny-side-up eggs. He would start, with great exaggeration, 'You know, Bimal, today I was worried because first only air came.' Then he would go on to describe the entire episode to me. I had to cling on to all my cadet training where I had rolled in cow dung, went to camps, and managed a lot of things with very little water, to keep a straight face and continue eating my breakfast. It wasn't an interesting event to experience when I was trying to get my sustenance, but it was hilarious when I wrote about it later.

Until then, I had never realised that I enjoyed writing that much. It was a revelation to me, and I started writing even more. My sister, Minichechi, used to get a dose of my writing and she goaded me to write more. See, this is why you need sisters. It's always good for your morale to keep a couple of them around, you see. I wish I had all the papers in which I wrote about so many of my life incidents. It really was interesting (at least at the time of writing, it was. To me). Maybe if I read them now, I might be aghast at what I thought was writing at that time.

I also remembered that one of the things that kept me going through my cadet training days, what kept me awake through some (most, actually) of the lectures I had to attend was writing letters while the rest of the class slept. In a day, I used to write about two or three letters, not the inland ones that took a mere five minutes to finish, but pages and pages about all that was happening to me and us as cadets. I started the same thing again. During my hospital stay, I wrote reams and reams about all the interesting and not-so-interesting things that were happening at the hospital.

That was the time one of my coursemates, Kalyan, came to Kolkata. A delightful chap, always happy and smiling. He also played the guitar and we used to jam together at times. We had performed together many times as well in our cadet's music band named 'Log-a-Rhythm'. A smart name for a techie music band, right?

What I did not know was the fact that Kolkata happened to be the place where the Givson guitars were manufactured. To my ultimate joy and surprise, he turned up at my bedside with a shining, new, acoustic guitar. I was so happy to see him with the guitar. When I look back, I feel that the guitar was one of the best and most appropriate gifts that I have received in my lifetime. I never learned to play the guitar formally. I was, and still am, self-taught. The challenge with self-learning is that there is an initial period which is very frustrating to the learner and even more irritating to the listener. At least the learner has the hope that one day he would be able to play it properly. I still don't see any silver lining for the listeners. Luckily, I had crossed that stage during the final year of cadet training. Since I was the 'senior coursemate', the poor guys tolerated me somehow. I am pretty sure that my original coursemates would have kicked my butt for making such horrible noises from such a beautiful instrument.

The guitar became my 'go-to' equipment at the hospital from then on. Reading, writing, and playing the guitar were how I spent my days for a long time. It created a very nice ambience at the hospital too. I was in intensive care, which comprised four beds right next to the nurses' station. The patients who needed constant and regular check-ups and care were kept here. I had three more retired officers who were localites[22] along with me in the room. They were good-natured and talked all day long. Post lunch, they used to tell me, 'Bimal, *kuch baja yaar.*' (Bimal, please play something,

---

[22]A native or resident of the locality under consideration. In this case, they were all based in Kolkata city

friend) I used to play and sing Kishoreda[23] songs and they were happy. There were no smartphones or internet at the time where I could learn and play more. Otherwise, I think I would've become an ace guitar player because I had so much time at hand and so few things to do. I had to replay the songs I knew and try and figure out new songs on my own.

The next thing I did at the hospital was to make a sincere effort to make friends there. Many young army officers had come in from the Northeast and almost all of them had had direct interactions with terrorists. I loved listening to their stories about these encounters, their life in forward areas, their hopes, their dreams, and their aspirations. Despite the seriousness of my accident, I felt embarrassed about it because every young army officer admitted was there because of a bullet injury, mine blast, ambush and stuff like that and I was the only one with a 'bike accident'. I have always maintained that whatever pay these young people at the front are given is way too less for the kind of service they provide. How can you put a price on someone's life? That is why it is called 'service'. It has always been a service to my country.

This was also the time when the surgeon realised that my wound (or whatever it was) was not healing. I was promptly sent for another surgery of skin grafting where some layers of skin from my left thigh were removed and put over the wound. All of us prayed for it to work and for my leg to accept this skin as its own. Thankfully it did. That night was also very bad. Earlier, it was only my right leg which was hurting but now my left thigh also got involved. It was as if someone had ripped off my skin (that *is* what happened, even though it was done surgically) and the pain was excruciating. Once that also became slightly better, my external fixators were removed,

---

[23] Kishore Da or Kishore Kumar was an Indian playback singer, musician and actor. He is widely regarded as one of the greatest, most influential and dynamic singers in the history of Indian music.

and a full-length plaster was put in with a huge window cut out from the cast for cleaning and dressing my wound. It even had a wooden heel fixed to the plaster so that I didn't need separate footwear. I was thrilled because I was now able to walk around with crutches. This was a big improvement from walking around with fixators using a walker. It was very tricky as I had to take utmost care that I did not hit or even touch the fixators anywhere, as that caused me to scream in pain.

Conversations are not just great for passing time, they are also great for healing. It was horrible when I was alone and the only conversation I had was with God and that too mostly accusatory in nature. It only made me feel worse about myself and my future. When we talk to others, we are not only dissipating the effect of whatever has happened to us, but we also get to know about their trials and tribulations, which may give us a very different perspective on our own thought process.

❊❊❊

There is a lot more that happened at the hospital, both good and bad. Those two years in the hospital changed my life forever. It also made me a better person. Someone who understood pain and helplessness, someone who had to fight physical, mental, and emotional demons all alone and learnt how to survive through the worst that had happened. I became more patient, kinder, and someone who could empathize with others. To sum it up, it gave me a lot of internal strength.

It is true what they say, *'What doesn't kill you makes you stronger.'* I learnt this every single day at the three different hospitals that I was in (Vizag hospital, Kolkatta and the last 6 months at Pune ortho speciality hospital). I went through the worst summer in

Kolkata (in 40 years) on the top floor of the hospital with a full-length plaster and found it amusing to sit with a wet towel over my body instead of a shirt and joke about it. I learned that there are very few delights that can match the ones I got when I was able to reach a very itchy spot on my leg inside the plaster with the help of a fully opened shirt hanger. I was able to get into the good books of all the nursing staff and they connected with me so well that all of them started getting food for me from their homes and one of them even got me food from her hostel. I went through a bad bout of chicken pox in the middle of all these, while I was in the hospital and went through a period of total isolation, another great learning experience.

I was even able to get back on my feet quickly, when another tragedy struck me. At the end of almost two long years of hospitalisation, I was all ready to go back and do my Marine Engineering Specialisation course. In the discharge medical board, my medical category was not upgraded. I was confused and met the Surgeon Colonel. He gave me the news that my condition would not only never improve but would keep deteriorating and would likely culminate in a hip replacement surgery sometime in the near future and that I could never go back on board ships. I remember breaking down badly in front of my friends at the hospital because I had kept my spirits up all this while, looking at the goal of completing my specialisation. I not only had planned but took action towards it as well because I was really looking forward to getting back to operational Navy. That night was bad, but I quickly rebounded and in two days, I was 'back on my feet', mentally and emotionally.

All this clarity of thought came about only because I was willing to step outside my situation and look at things objectively. When I did that, everything changed, even though nothing around me was in a good place. I had just learned that my medical condition would only get worse. My career just got thrown out of the window and life took another sudden turn towards uncertainty.

The only thing that changed was how I saw things. When my perception and my internal conversation changed about all that was happening, my entire world changed. It was like someone switching on a bright light in a dark room. I could see everything clearly and for what it was, and not as some huge and vindictive cosmic plot against me.

When I look back and try to see how this happened and try to put a logical sense to it, I realised that through trial and error, I had applied some very practical and systematic approaches to my situation.

Summing it up:

1. First and the most important step was for me to take responsibility for the situation that I was in. I'm not saying in any way that the accident was my fault and that is something I guess I will never know since I decided not to pursue the case. I am talking about the responsibility for my well-being, both mentally and emotionally.
2. I stopped being a victim who has been betrayed, let down, been given an unfair deal in life, because I looked at the facts and the stories that I was making up regarding the incident. The facts were simple and straight: I met with an accident, had to go through multiple operations, and now, I was recovering. The recovery time would be long since it was a major accident. However, the worst was over (at least for the time being). The stories I made up were better than a lot of Bollywood thrillers and I was living in that story. I was judging and seeing everything through those coloured glasses.

3. I stopped living in the past glory of what all I was on the verge of accomplishing (like the software that I had built).
4. I stopped living in the future, planning my date of discharge, my courses, et cetera as I had no idea how long I was going to be there.
5. I looked at what was in my control and what was not in my control. The only thing that was in my control was how I could spend each day.
6. I started taking things one day at a time. I looked at what best could be done every single day and focused on that.
7. I looked at what skills I could learn while I was in the hospital. The only things I could do were learn to be a better guitar player and a slightly better writer. Everything was through trial and error as there was no one to guide me or correct me.
8. I started focusing on what veterans talked about and advised about. My whole journey as a parenting coach started on this hospital bed, that too thanks to two officers who were admitted next to me (more on this later). They gave me a new perspective and I realigned my priorities in life.
9. I made as many friends as I could with fellow patients, nursing staff and anyone else who were willing to speak to me.
10. I trusted in the higher intelligence of God. I realised that there had to be a plan for me in this life and I should let it unfold as per the universe's plan. I knew that He would never put me through something that I was not capable of handling.

In conclusion to this episode of my life, what I want to share is something that I learned from Tony Robbins[24]. 'Nothing in my life has any meaning other than the meaning I give it.' (From *Awaken*

---

[24]Anthony Jay Robbins is an American author, coach, speaker, and philanthropist. He is known for his infomercials, seminars, and self-help books including the books *Unlimited Power* and *Awaken the Giant Within*.

the Giant Within). I have heard multiple versions of it in various forums as well as from different people.

You can apply all the things I've listed above to any situation that you have faced, or may face in your life. If you are willing to step outside the story that you have made up and are willing to look at the incident objectively, it will become easy to apply all these steps or principles (of the 'What Next Method') and everything will change for you.

Know that you are given only those challenges that you can handle. At times it may not appear so, but it is the truth. You always have two choices: you can either succumb to it or come out a victor, a warrior, and not only become stronger mentally and emotionally, but you will be able to help many others who haven't had the experiences that you went through and are perplexed and bewildered at all that is happening to them.

Remember, *what doesn't kill you, only makes you stronger!*[25]

The time spent in the hospital was very tough—physically, mentally, and emotionally—for me. However, at times, something so good happens after a tough phase in life where you feel that *maybe I had to go through all the tough times so that I could have this.* That is exactly what happened to me after this.

---

[25]This comes from an aphorism of the 19th century German philosopher Friedrich Nietzsche. It has been translated into English and quoted in several variations

CHAPTER 8

LOVE IS A SMOKE

'I think someone is J[26],' she said and winked at me with a sweet smile.

We were standing at an internet café just outside the gate of INS Hamla, which is the logistics training centre for the Navy. I just couldn't believe my luck. For me, it wasn't love at first sight, since I had seen her a couple of times at the café, but I was fascinated. I wanted to get to know her somehow.

INS Hamla happens to be one of the most beautiful Naval bases. It is situated in the north-western part of Mumbai on Marve beach, very near Madh Island on Malad West. The Officers' mess and a large part of Officers' accommodations are situated right on the beach and the entire base is alongside. It is not a very huge base like Shivaji, and I could see the sea from almost anywhere in the base. Even those who's never been fitness enthusiasts turned into beach runners in Hamla. It has a private beach exclusively for the base. No visitors are allowed, making it a very clean and serene place. I used to wake up to the sound of fishing boats passing by and seagulls screaming. I have never stayed so close to the beach even when I visited Goa. It also had some lovely shacks which were right on the beach. If we were lucky, we could get glimpses of celebrities coming to spend a weekend in the shacks.

---

[26] J – Meaning jealous

How I reached there is another story.

I had to change my branch since I had not completed Engine Room Watchkeeping, even though my Commander(E) tried his best with the authorities. I had to complete a few more weeks on board to be considered for that. I was given the option to change my branch from Engineering to either Logistics or Provost (Naval Police). I chose Logistics as many further options could become available to me going forward.

Once out of the hospital, I moved back to INS Shivaji and joined as Assistant Mess Secretary. What was I doing back at Shivaji? I had mentioned that I had not only planned but also took action. During my initial plans to complete my Marine Engineering Specialisation, I had decided that I would do other courses first and complete my Watchkeeping at the end by which time I would become fit to go to sea. This plan translated into action as I was nearing my discharge from the hospital. I wrote a letter to the Department of Personnel, which handles the transfers and postings in the Navy, requesting them to send me to Shivaji once I was out of the hospital. They were kind enough to get me posted there. At that time, I didn't know that I couldn't continue in the engineering branch.

Once I was there, the only duty I could discharge was that of the Assistant Mess Secretary. It was a great tenure as my Mess Secretary was my NEC Senior and a very jovial person. I was waiting for my orders to join the Sub Lieutenant Logistics course, which was a 7-month course for people who were getting into the logistics branch. I received the order to join the course and I shifted to INS Hamla in Dec 1999. My batch was very small. It comprised of three Indian Navy officers (including me), one lady officer from the Coast Guard and two Nigerian officers. We had a pretty good time together there.

We still did not have the concept of mobile phones or even the internet. That is the time I saw an internet café just outside the gate of Hamla and I became a regular visitor there after dinner for about an hour. I browsed the net occasionally, and when I got bored, got on ICQ chat, which was the closest thing to social media at the time. You login to a chat, which was DOS-based, meaning one could only communicate through words. No images, smileys, emojis, nothing. The standard opening line was 'a/s/l please' which translates to 'age/sex/location'. The few that were there of the opposite sex hardly responded and I used to wonder why, until one day, I got bored out of my skull and logged in as a female. Even before I could look at the list of other people who were in the 'room', I was inundated with asl requests from at least 50 people there. From then on, whenever I finished my quota of browsing and chatting, I would log in as a girl. It was interesting to see how some were nice and courteous, some were cheesy, and some were outright horrible. I felt bad for all the girls who were on the chat (I mean the real ones).

Since I became a regular at the café, I became friends with the young guy running the place. We used to sit and talk a lot and I even met some of his friends who used to visit the café and he would introduce all of them to me enthusiastically. One day, I saw him standing outside and talking to a beautiful young girl. After she left, I asked him who she was, and he just dismissed me saying that she was just a friend who comes there at times. I could sense his reluctance to give me more details. I decided to try again later. As luck would have it, she was back the same week. I was sitting inside, surfing the net and she was talking to my owner-friend. I decided to seize the opportunity and went outside. I started talking to my friend with the girl standing right next to him. She was smiling at me. I was smiling at her. But my friend, unlike the other times when he promptly introduced me to his friends, did not show any interest in doing the same with her. Finally, I got tired of it, and I introduced myself to her. And then with a sheepish grin and lame apology, he reluctantly introduced her to me. She smiled and said, 'Hi! I'm June.'

We got on very well and she was easy to talk to. She told me that she had just finished her 12th, which turned out to be a lie. She revealed much later that she didn't want me to think of her as too young for me. Since my friend did not show any interest in introducing us, we didn't feel obligated to include him in our conversations going forward. We used to sit outside the café and chat while he kind of glared at me (or her since he knew her longer than I did). We exchanged numbers (landline, of course) and we started hanging out every evening. We went to movies together, or sometimes to the beach and just sat there or went to this awesome ice cream parlour, Sanchas, which had very yummy ice creams. She stayed very close to Hamla with her elder sister (who was younger than me). Her uncle who lived nearby was their local guardian as her parents were abroad. It gave us a lot of freedom to be out of home for long durations, even late nights, but I had to make sure that her sister was informed. She was quite cool with me as we too became good friends quickly.

As we spent more time together, we kind of knew we were made for each other (Yeah. Happens. Don't laugh). My only concern was that I was a born-again Christian since my second year of cadets training at NEC. My faith was strong, and I had no intention of changing it/discarding it even for someone I loved a lot.

One day, the topic did come up, and I confessed to her about my peculiar belief in Christianity, and to my utter surprise, it turned out that she and her whole family were born-again Christians. I didn't need any further proof that we belonged together. What were the chances that of all the people I met, I end up with the one from the small percentage of people who were following the same faith that I was? I was looking for a place of worship on Sundays and she knew one. We started going there together. She introduced me to her friends and acquaintances over there and they all became like an extended family to me.

When I give, I give unconditionally. I kind of get consumed in giving all that I have. This, to me, was the first real 'love affair' that was very serious. I had just come out of a near-death scenario, spent two years in a hospital looking at walls and beds and people in pain all around. My dream career had come to a grinding halt, my leg was totally disfigured, I had pus coming out of a tiny hole in my leg at times, and I could not run around or even walk without a slight limp. I had given up my hopes on any possibility of a romance or love affair in my life and I had a girl that I would consider impossible in all respects even for a normally good-looking and well-functioning man. She was young, beautiful, sexy, and well-spoken, born and bred in Mumbai, the land of the ultra-modern girls. I felt that all the pain and suffering that I had gone through in the last couple of years were just for this gift... and it was worth everything that I had to go through. I knew that we would get married and live happily ever after and I was prepared to do whatever it took to make sure it happened.

It is true when they say that love is blind. You miss a lot of things that would have caught your attention if you had observed and evaluated objectively. For example, to all *my* friends, she was my fiancée (she insisted to be introduced as one) but to all *her* friends, I was her 'friend' (which I didn't mind that time). She met all my friends and batchmates, I met just one or two of her friends. I could not pick her up in front of her college. I had wait slightly away from the entrance. She would walk there and then we could leave. All these details were of significance, but I realised this only much later.

I guess I was also quite protective of her for multiple reasons. She was much younger than me, she was living alone just with her sister, her parents were separated, and she also had a lot of insecurities about herself and things around her. I was also coming from a place of insecurities that I had due to all the events that had happened in my life in a previous couple of years. Because of this, I suppose, after my stint at the hospital, my tolerance and patience levels were very high. After a few months, her mother did come down to spend some time with her daughters, and I connected and bonded with her very well (which also became an issue with her as she thought I was trying to steal her mother from her).

There was no plan or requirement to meet her dad. It was like a dream coming true for me. I was a little worried about my parents since she was very young and very different from how we were as a family. I was very reluctant to tell them about June for a long time and I only did when we decided to get married. I was not sure how they would react but to my pleasant surprise, my parents were more concerned about my happiness than theirs (how are they so wise?). They did not have any issues as long as I was clear and sure about the girl that she was the one I wanted to spend the rest of my life with.

Basically, they put the responsibility for my decision squarely on my shoulders. And like every other time, I should have done my due diligence and looked at everything that happened and was happening using logic and common sense. Unfortunately, these are brain functions and I never used anything but my heart when it came to this girl. I had not even realised that I had alienated myself from any kind of social life as my only aim in life became spending time with her after my classes while I was at Hamla. It didn't matter that once I started working, I was located at the other end of Mumbai. I used to finish work, change, and ride my bike across the city. Due to this daily routine, I had no time for anything in the evening, not even to meet my coursemates who were posted in Mumbai.

Coursemates are never lost because we bond for life. Just that once I moved out of the Engineering branch, I was following a different path compared to the others. All my coursemates were posted on board ships. The first posting is always a 'field posting' and for us, it was ships. I did not even have time to catch up with whoever was in Mumbai at the time. I missed get-togethers, birthday parties and every other occasion that warranted me to choose between my friends and my 'love'. I was consumed with this entire affair I was having with this girl. Nothing and no one else mattered. Even though I teach about toxic relationships now, I had no idea what one looked like at the time.

Another very interesting aspect of our relationship was that it was almost a secret one. None of her friends or acquaintances met me more than once and even the ones who did, didn't know me as her fiancée. However, it didn't matter to me as her family knew me and had met me, and more than anything, people in our church knew about us as a couple who were soon to get married. At the church, I was drawn towards the worship team (something like a choir but more like a band in our case) and wanted to be a part of it. She could sing a bit. So, she was also very keen to be a part of it.

The worship team was a group of youngsters, most of them were my age or younger than me, and we bonded well. It was led by our youth leader who was deeply spiritual, and he had a godly voice. When he used to sing while playing his keyboard, I could feel a connection with God. He had that effect not just on me but on every single person in the audience. He was like an idol to all of us and we started hanging out a lot together, attending youth camps at Lonavala and other places. For me, it was the perfect place to be.

One of the things that June always used to tell me from very early on was how much she had missed having a brother to take care of her, to listen to her and to advise her in life. I was filling the role of 'all-in-one' for her. When we started spending more time with the worship team, I got close to the worship leader as we had a lot of mutual respect, and he was guiding me as well as her about music and life in general. He took on the role of her brother and I was thrilled that finally she got what she wanted in life. He was the one person I confided in, about the two of us, which made him the only other person who really knew how close we were and what our plans were for our lives. I encouraged her as well to confide in him.

Two years had passed since the time I first met her, and we had had our ups and downs. I had figured out that it wasn't going to be easy, but I had made up my mind to go all the way in this relationship. The time had come to take it to the next level. I had my leave coming up and I had to tell my parents about it. Her mother was in Mumbai, and she also said that she might come to visit my parents to plan and formalize the next steps in our lives. I was ecstatic as I went home and told my parents for the first time about her and the fact that we intended to get married.

My dad was more concerned about how the house looked. It had been a while since it was painted and with all the rains in Kerala, the paint tends to wear off pretty quickly. His focus then was to get the house in a presentable condition and went in search of a good painter who could finish the work before her mom came to visit us in the next couple of weeks.

One of the important and favourite things that I always did during my holidays was to visit my cousin Preethichechi, Unniyettan and my nieces. They lived in a different city. I had mentioned that no visit to Kerala was complete without a visit to their home. I think one of the reasons for this was also the 4 to 5-hour drive to their home, right through the heart of Kerala.

Such a drive, even now, always rejuvenates me. I did not want to break the routine and went to my cousin's home for a week to spend time with them and my nieces. I had given the landline number to June to make sure that she could reach me irrespective of where I was. My days there were filled with lots of games and Malayalam comedy movies during the day and ended with some sumptuous meals prepared specially for me by Preechechi (as I called her). Days passed like this, and one night after dinner, we were just sitting and chatting happily, and Preechechi was in the kitchen when she called out and said I had a call. Initially, I thought it was from my parents asking me to come back home.

It was June. For the first time, she sounded very formal. She just told me that it was not working for her, and she was breaking up. She told me that she has sent an email with more details in it and the line went dead. I realised that I did not even get a chance to respond or ask a question during the two-minute call that she made.

I just stood there numb, not able to process what I had just heard. My nieces were tugging at my hand asking me to get back into jokes and conversations. I had no intention of ruining their joy and excitement and I just went through the motions that evening. I could not call her back as my cousin did not have STD on their phone. If you are wondering how a phone could have STD, let me assure you that, unlike today, the commonly accepted full form for

STD during our time was 'Subscriber Trunk Dialling' which simply meant the add-on facility that had to be bought from the telephone provider, to make interstate calls.

The conversation with June hit me hard, especially once I was in bed and everyone else had slept. I just could not make any sense of what had just happened. We were together for more than two years. I had always bent backwards to do things for her. She did not tell me there was an issue. Her sister liked me a lot, her mother loved me and thought I was perfect for her daughter. I had thanked God for all the troubles I went through with the accident and at the hospital because without that incident and so much time at the hospital, I would have never met her. I went through our conversations from the previous six months at least to see where this was coming from, and I drew a blank. I could not sleep that night, but I could not even cry because of my nieces. Could it be an elaborate prank? She did not sound how she would normally and deep inside I knew she meant what she said.

It was very frustrating and upsetting when I couldn't find a reason for it. I had gone through the same feeling during my accident as well, not finding any logical reason and remaining frustrated until I surrendered to whatever process I was being taken through. In this case, the only thing I could hope for was to get back to my city and find an internet café so that I could check the email that she had sent me. There was only one issue with that because there was a *hartal*[27] in Kerala (which is very common) and there were no buses (I had taken a bus this time to visit them) plying for the next couple of days.

The next few days were terrible. I just could not share anything with my cousins, definitely not with my nieces to whom I was a

---

[27] Hartal - (In South Asia) a closure of shops and offices as a protest or a mark of sorrow

source of joy and fun. I did my very best to keep a straight and happy face throughout while internally being in total turmoil. Finally, after about three days, the *hartal* was over, and I took the first bus back to my city. I was desperate for answers because I was trying to figure out what could have gone wrong and what could be the reason for her to say things like that and I kept drawing a blank every single time. I was sure that once I read her email, I would know how to fix things so that we could get back together. This had to be some silly misunderstanding of sorts and nothing more.

I reached home to find my home in a mess because my father had started painting the house with gusto. I just borrowed the keys to the scooter and went looking for a good internet café to solve this puzzle. Finally, I found one, some distance away from my home. I took the token for an hour and told them I might need an extension as there was something very important to be sorted. I went to my cubicle, logged in to the internet and opened my email. There was an email from her which just had a cold 'Hi' in the subject line. With my heart pounding hard with anxiety, I clicked the email open.

The email was not a long-drawn one with explanations and an apology (something that one would expect when there is a breakup after more than two years of courtship). It was just two lines, to be precise. It said how she had grand plans for her life and how she could not see me 'fit' in her grand plans, with the standard assurance that I would get someone much better and more suited for me.

I just sat there, re-reading the email multiple times hoping that somehow the entire content would change magically to how and when we should get married. Nothing happened for over 30 mins, and I was just sitting there, staring at the email. I was trying hard to hold back my emotions that were threatening to burst. The one thing that I was holding on to, the one thing that had helped me justify all the pain that I had suffered, was gone. It was as if someone had pulled the carpet from under my feet. I didn't reply to the cashier who looked concerned at the way my face had changed from the time I came in and got up to ask if I was all right and if I needed anything. I think I just waved him off.

Somehow, I managed to reach home without another accident (as I was not paying attention to anything that I did. Neither my driving nor the traffic). I just went into my room and shut myself in. I could not sit, I could not stand, I could not lie down. I was not worried about what I would tell my parents. My mother somehow hadn't been very thrilled with the fact that she was far too young and for my dad, any excuse to get the house painted was good enough. It was not about anyone else. I just could not handle the emotional pain I was going through. The stint in the hospital was more physical and mental for me, and even though a lot of emotions were involved, my heart had never hurt like this ever before. I felt as if my heart was crumbling inside my chest.

I tried calling her back since our phone had an STD facility. She just refused to even come on the phone and talk to me. I called my close friend, Harish, who was also posted in Mumbai and was living across my room in the officer's mess, just like in our cadet days. He knew about us and used to attend the same church as well. He just told me to come back as there were things that he wanted to talk to me about. In the few days that remained of my leave, I again tried to go through every single incident and interaction to figure out what could have prompted her to take such a decision. I had always been there for her every single need, every single day (except when I was on duty). I just could not understand what could have gone so wrong that she ended our courtship of more than two years through a phone call that was less than two minutes in length.

My leave had become agonisingly painful, and I just needed to go back. I still clung to the hope that all I had to do was sit with her and find out what she was upset about. I was still quite confident that I would be able to 'fix' it. There had to be some misunderstanding that I could sort out.

On top of it all, I knew for a fact that God would never be so inhuman to me. He had put me through the worst physical and mental pain just a couple of years ago and he was rewarding me with this 'lovely' relationship for all that I had endured. Why would he hammer me down with something that would break me emotionally as well? I was quite sure of God's justice that way.

I reached Mumbai, dumped my bag and went straight to Harish's cabin. It was locked as he was out for some work. The only thing I could do was wait. I could have taken my bike and gone to her house to ask her for an explanation. I held myself back because Harish had told me that there was something important that he wanted to talk to me about. I wanted to get the full picture before doing anything.

I just waited in my room in agony and anticipation. Harish came to my room in the evening. He sat on the chair opposite to mine and said in the gentlest voice, 'Beems, it's not just that she has broken up with you, she is also getting married.'

My mind just exploded, and I shouted, 'What? When did this happen? I was away for just a couple of weeks. Who is she getting married to? Who told you all this?'

All that I had bottled up inside started exploding out of me in a desperate attempt to make sense of all that he was telling me.

He again very gently shared the name of the guy she was getting married to and added that everyone knew about this. All the agitation, exasperation, and frustration that were ready to come out of me suddenly stopped midway. It was as if I had suddenly entered the eye of a storm. He just held my shoulder and said, 'I'm sorry' and left.

I relived the moments when I was told about the relegation during my cadet days. Here also, I was numb for a few minutes, my mind going totally blank. When I came to my senses, I still couldn't fathom what I had just heard. It made no logical sense to me. She was getting married to the worship and youth leader in the church.

He had been like a brother to her and he had even declared it openly to the elders of the church. More than anything, he was one of the few people with whom I shared everything about us, which meant he knew how much we loved each other (I mean how much I loved her) and what she meant for me. He was like a brother to me. He would never do something like this to me. How could he? I fought with the information that I got from Harish, trying desperately to find facts and the hope that this was all a huge misunderstanding and nothing else.

Your mind is a genius. Even in the chaos, if you ask it, it will show you the truth. Suddenly, all the time when I had had a gut feeling that something was wrong was brought back to focus. Then and there, I started to see all that I had chosen to ignore until then. The signs were all there in front of me. I had just chosen to ignore all of them because maybe I was too much in love with her, maybe I trusted both too much, maybe I wanted it to work so badly that I was willing to ignore all that was happening right in front of my eyes.

❋❋❋

In the evening, I was sitting at the Naval bar, nursing a drink. I decided to call him instead of her. I thought he might have the courage or at least the basic courtesy to talk to me, man-to-man. He picked up my call and I just asked him a simple question, 'Brother, how could you do this to me? After knowing everything, after spending so much time with me, after declaring her as your sister in front of the church, how could you do this?'

After a few seconds of silence, he said in a feeble voice, 'I am really sorry about this.'

Whoa! He was sorry! So that makes everything fine, I suppose. I was not done yet. I wanted one more vital piece of information. More than information, I needed confirmation because once the fog lifted, I was able to see a lot of things that happened for what it truly was, without them being marred by my need for it to be the way I wanted it to be. I asked him just one more question. 'Who proposed?'

My guess was spot-on. I thanked him for taking my call and answering my queries and I cut the call.

My desperation, my hurt, everything that I had felt for her and towards this incident now turned into one big ball of anger towards her. For cheating on me, for being manipulative, for lying about so many things, for treating me the way she treated me (I deserved it because I let her do all that, but wait... that realisation came later).

❖ ❖ ❖

Now that the news had been broken to me, she was okay to respond to my messages after my phone call to the worship leader. I don't remember her saying even once that she was sorry about anything. Now, I was like an animal that was deeply wounded. I just wanted to retaliate and hurt her back with the same intensity. I told her about all the things that I had held back in my mind during all the times when I felt she was being insensitive and mean to me. It was of no use at this stage, but at least I was getting the pleasure of telling her those things to her face (on phone actually). I was so hurt that I even demanded that she return all the money that she had taken from me in the form of gifts and loans, which was quite a substantial amount. I forced her to commit to repayment of the money at the earliest, which I knew she couldn't do and at some level, I felt happy that I was causing her this humiliation.

After a day or so, once my anger settled down to manageable levels, I realised that my peace was totally disturbed. I have always been a peace-loving person and I knew that when I am angry or upset with someone else, more than the other person, *I* suffered the most. The same was happening here in this case as well. I may have spoken and done a lot of things in a fit of anger and hurt, but fundamentally, I had lost my peace and I was full of negativity. I didn't like being in this state at all. So, I had to ask myself the inevitable question, *'What Next?'*

I had to again work my way through the process and figure out what was in my control and what wasn't.

I realised that at some level, I was still trying to turn things around and make her realise what all and how much I had done for her. I was so desperate that I had stooped to the level of taking stock of the money that I had spent on her. I had to accept the fact that was staring me in the face, that she didn't love me, that she didn't want me. This was the toughest pill to swallow as my fear of not being loved by anyone after my accident resurfaced. I knew that there was no one to help me in this situation. I had to fight this demon and come out of it on my own.

It is interesting to see what happens the moment you are ready to take full responsibility for your actions. All the bullshit goes away. Maybe not all, but you start seeing with more clarity. I realised to my surprise that at some level, I was glad that this had happened. All the hurt, all the let-downs, all the bad treatment from her had accumulated inside, maybe at a subconscious level. I realised that I was angrier at the fact that I was betrayed by a man who called himself her brother and was my biggest support in this entire 'affair'.

I also realised that if I wanted to be truly peaceful, I had to totally 'let go' of her, of him, and I had to come to a stage where I was able to wish them well and mean it. It did take me a couple of days and a lot of time in prayer. But once I knew deep in my spirit that whatever happened was for my own good (though I could not explain it logically at the time), I could really let go. The moment I truly let go, I realised that in my anger, I was trying to hurt someone whom I had loved very deeply just a few weeks before. What I needed was to be thankful for all the good times that we did share, and to be happy that she is happy (not in a Devdas[28] way, but genuinely). The two years that I spent with her prepared me to be a better person.

After about 4 or 5 days, when I fully reconciled with the reality, I called both of them and wished them a happy married life together.

The transition wasn't easy at all. I had let go of my anger and frustration and the need to get back at them. I managed to let go of all that from my heart. However, the hurt remained and unfortunately, was very visible to everyone, especially those in the church. I did not complain to anyone, I did not tell them anything,

---

[28]Devdas is a fictional character in Indian literature who descents into alcoholism, ultimately leading to his emotional deterioration and him seeking refuge with a courtesan because he did not get the love of his life.

but the elders of the church put their foot down. Everyone knew that we were a couple who were going to get married very soon. More than that, the guy was the youth worship leader for the church and had declared in front of all of them that she was like his sister.

Obviously, that was not the right kind of modelling the church needed at that time. The elders of the church said that they can't get married. I even called one of the elders and assured them that I did not have any issue with their marriage or whatever they had decided to do, but it was not just about me by then. I came to know later that they both ran away from Mumbai and the church, and got married. It was just another piece of news or gossip to me by then.

While I was hurting inside (which was visible to everyone around me), one event happened that totally changed my perspective and healed me like magic. I did not have too many coursemates with me in Mumbai after shifting to Logistics. I had a couple of friends, but they did not know the depth and intensity of what I had shared with June. Harish gave me spiritual advice, which kept my faith going strong, but did not do much to heal the raw wound. In the congregation, there was a couple, Rajeev and Perola, whose house I used to visit for my midweek prayer meetings. They both were doing very well for themselves, had a lovely family and had two kids. Rajeev was someone I looked up to. Even though he was older than me, he was always kind and compassionate and was more like a friend, guide and advisor to us, the youngsters.

One day, out of the blue, he invited me over to lunch at his place after Sunday service. I did not have anything planned for Sundays. Earlier, all my days revolved around June and suddenly, I had a lot of free time on hand. I was happy to spend some time with them. There was a good spread at home as if the invite was pre-planned. We had a sumptuous lunch after which we sat down for general chitchat in the living room. Perola gave me a large bowl of ice cream and quietly left the room leaving just us men to talk to each other. Rajeev began to talk about his life and his younger days and to my shock and horror, he told me about how he also had gone through something very similar.

I don't remember the exact story now. What I do remember is how I felt. I was sitting with someone whom I looked up to, someone who had a wonderful family, someone who was doing well in life and someone who seemed really content with his life. I was under the impression that my days of happiness were over. The hope that I would ever fall in love was dismissed and I believed that the dark cloud on top of my head would never disperse.

All this information meant that I was not the only person who had suffered like this. This meant that I was not really a bad person. More than anything, I realised that this was not the end of my happiness. It was possible to have a happy life and family despite all that happened to me. This was a total revelation to me. I, for some reason, had never even considered the possibility that these things do happen to other people as well, to good people, and here was living proof that it was possible. He even confessed that he was much happier and a more fulfilled man after the other girl had left him.

This was one of the biggest learnings of my life. Seek help. Especially from people you look up to. You may be thinking, 'Duh! What is so path-breaking about this? It's something very basic.' Yes, it may be basic from an external perspective, but when you are in the middle of it, it is quite possible that you can't think or see beyond what you are going through. The fact is that most people have gone through what you have gone through or are going through. The intensity may vary. That's all. I walked home a completely changed man that day. I realised that I was holding on to the hurt and betrayal only because once I let go of it, I had to take full responsibility. I could not be the 'poor me, look at me' person anymore. I never was that type of person, but this was more for internal validation than for getting any external sympathy from others. This incident truly healed me. I did not have the hurt, pain, and anger within me anymore.

I was free.

Looking back, I thank God for all that happened. The fact was that we would not have survived even a year as a married couple. It was not because of how she was. It was just that we were fundamentally very different people.

We both are happily married to our respective spouses as of today, and we are quite cordial with each other, which I think is great. In retrospect, June's words about me finding a better life partner did come true. My wife, Pallavi, and I have been happily married for about two decades now (more about this later).

Why did I share this incident with you? Most people have a failed love story in their lives. Or at least an infatuation that never became a reality. When we go through it, we feel as if no one can understand what we are going through. The hurt is deep, and the emotions are very high. My mentor, Blair Singer[29], always says, *'When emotions are high, intelligence is low.'* This is such a true statement and is the most applicable in cases like this where the heart is deeply involved.

Let me share some of the things I learned once I was out of the so-called 'trance' we think of as love. These advices are not just for men, but equally applicable to both genders because I have seen

---

[29]Blair Singer is a world-renowned speaker and the bestselling author of *Little Voice Mastery, SalesDogs* and *Team Code of Honor*.

these behaviours in both. Both come from a common breed of "idiots" or as my friend calls them, *Chaman*[30].

Summing up:

1. Trust yourself and your gut. God has blessed us with a powerful tool called intuition. Most of the time, we recognise and give it credit only in retrospect, like I did. You don't really have to do the same. If you 'feel' that something is not right and if you get that 'feeling' multiple times, nine times out of ten, your feeling will be right. Take action to mitigate the feeling. Don't shove it under the rug.
2. Don't ever accept two different rules when it comes to commitment. One person cannot be a 'fiancée' while the other person remains a 'friend' to the same set of people. It makes no logical sense at all, but some of you may not realise it when you are in the thick of things.
3. Respect yourself first. If you won't respect yourself, don't expect anyone else to do the same with you. Don't defend the disrespect/humiliation from your partner in the name of love. It is a sure recipe for disaster. Remember *"No one can ride your back unless it's bent"*. Make sure you have a spine and that it's not all packed up inside your brain.
4. For heaven's sake, have friends around. Not the formal ones. The ones who are willing to get in your bad books to make sure that you don't fall into a well. In most cases, your close friends can see what you can't see even if it is in front of your face. *Listen to them.* I am not saying to do exactly what they tell you to do but consider what they say and be willing to assess and judge without being blinded by emotions. Be objective.
5. Have some people to talk to and take advice from. These could be people you look up to. Someone who is living a life that

---

[30]Chaman is a hindi slang for idiot

you aspire for. Someone who has proven to be a reliable and trustworthy person over a period. Just don't sit and stew all alone. It doesn't help. It just doesn't.
6. If something goes wrong, be willing to look at things objectively. Be willing to separate facts from fiction, actual incidents from stories that you have made up.
7. More than anything else, have faith in God or the higher power. When you are in front of a mountain that looks impossible, you won't see the beautiful garden beyond the mountain where the higher power is trying to take you.

CHAPTER 9

AMOR FATI

The year 2003 was one of the best years of my life. I met my wife Pallavi (the one who was predicted to be 'better suited' for me). I met her when I was in no state or mood to be interested or involved with any woman after the fiasco with the last one, which was still very fresh. Incidentally, I found true love at the same place where I lost what I thought was true love. At the same church. God also has a great sense of humour. I still remember the first time I saw her. She was standing in line for the bread and wine (non-alcoholic, of course) that is shared by the pastor at the end of our service. I had got my share and I came out of the line and was looking casually at the people still in the line. My eyes fixed on her. She was wearing a pair of blue jeans and a white top. She had straight, flowing hair and blue eyes (yes, they were contact lenses). I didn't mean to stare but I think my eyes just refused to move beyond her. She saw me staring and instead of scowling, she gave me the brightest smile I had ever seen. I was pretty sure that she was smiling at someone next to me and I did look around. There was no one. When I looked back at her with pure disbelief, she smiled again. I smiled back but I think I was more nervous than happy.

From then on, Pal and I became acquaintances rather than friends. My interactions with her were more of the hello-and-goodbye kind. She was (and still is) a beauty, a true sight to behold. She could capture anyone's attention with just her eyes and smile. She looked too good to be true. I had decided that I did not want to get involved with any girl in the foreseeable future. So, for me, it was a *'Wow! What a gorgeous woman!'* distant observation (and appreciation of course), but nothing more. On top of that, I loved her name. Pallavi[31]. Not just for the meaning of it, but I had seen the Bollywood movie *Lamhe* during my cadet days and I just loved the lead actress Sridevi's name in that movie. Not just the name, but the whole first part between Viren (the lead actor) and Pallavi. It just happens to be one of my favourite movies.

By this time, I had made another couple of great friends at the church. They were a brother and sister duo, Latha and Prakash and much to my joy, were from Kerala. I did not leave or run away from the church, unlike my ex. Once my Logistics conversion course that I was undergoing at INS Hamla was complete, I was to get my first posting as a logistics officer. I got a call from one of my seniors, Vivek, who was also a great friend. He wanted to know if I was interested in staying in Mumbai. Logistics' postings can be tricky, and I knew I could get posted to any part of the country. I jumped at the opportunity and took it up. He told me that it's in the Base Victualling Yard. I didn't care what it was as long as it kept me in Mumbai. I had grown quite fond of Mumbai by then and was thrilled by the fact that I got a posting there itself, that too with an office very close to the officer's mess.

My joy was short-lived because I regretted the decision the moment I walked into my new 'office building'. It was more of a multi-storeyed warehouse for food. I did have a nice and spacious office, but everything outside it was nothing like what I thought

---

[31] The name Pallavi is primarily a female name of Indian origin that means "New Leaves". It is also the first stanza of a song which introduces the rest of the song.

I should be doing in life. I was standing in the middle of large heaps of sacks with rice, lentils, and all kind of dry ration. The ground floor was full of fruits and vegetables. All orders were in tonnes of quantities. It was everywhere and my job was to inspect these and decide if they met the required quality standards. I just couldn't digest it. After spending days and nights working with this marvellous device called the computer, this felt like going backwards by a hundred years. I did not even have a PC on my desk. Everything was on paper. By the end of the day, I used to be bored out of my wits doing the kind of work that did not hold my interest at all.

When you are forced to do something you are not interested in, I guess it will reflect on the quality of your work output. I remember my boss calling me twice to warn me about the quality of my output as well as my general interest, or the lack thereof, in the day-to-day activities at the yard.

I was clearly unhappy and by now I had learned that unhappiness is a result. It is never the cause. It was an indication for me to take stock of what was happening in my life. One day, I sat down in my room after dinner and did some digging into my mindset that was making me churn out sub-par work. I was never good at marketing myself (to be honest, I still am not) or promoting my work for others to notice, but I have never shied away from the work itself or put a half-hearted effort into anything that I took up. I just don't know how to do that. I used to get so consumed with my work that one of my friends used to tell me that I was very good at creating roots, but I also need to showcase the work that I put in.

Here, I was not even applying myself to learn the system and working hard towards making it better. That was never (and still is) not acceptable to me. Whether anyone noticed or not, I had to be sure that I was giving my everything to the work I was entrusted with. I realised that I was holding on to my computer software development experience that I had on board the ship. I had got even more attached to computers because when I was home on sick leave from the hospital, my brother-in-law had got me a state-of-the-art PC and I had spent a lot of time with it (mostly playing games). I had that PC in my room at the officer's mess as well. I had to let go of what I wanted to do and focus on what was there in front of me.

My boss, Captain Marya, was a maverick. He could get anything done for anyone. He had executed a couple of events for the Navy where he could get some Bollywood stars purely through his connections. He is the kind of boss anyone would love to have. He always had our backs. We could take executive decisions and he would support and stand by us. When I say 'us', it means Gautam and me, the two young officers who primarily ran the place. The total strength was four officers, including my boss. The third was the deputy to our boss and he was more into administration and management. The daily operations were run by the two of us, Gautam and me.

We were both lieutenants, unmarried and carefree. We could really apply ourselves to our jobs and make a difference in the place. We had to take instant decisions that involved tonnes of food items and lakhs of rupees. We were singlehandedly catering to the entire western fleet, all the establishments in Mumbai as well as all over Maharashtra. It was a lot of responsibility and there was a lot to do. When only two officers are handling all the operations, one of us just couldn't afford to slacken. I understood that there was so much I could do for the organization and the Navy if I took up the challenge and responsibility whole-heartedly. I also realised that the scale and impact of what I was doing there were much larger than what I had done with a computer program. I decided to embrace it with both hands.

The very next day, my office seemed different to me. Everything was the same, but nothing was the same for me. All it took was to do a hard audit of what was happening in my work and my approach to it. More importantly, I had to analyse what was happening to my attitude towards my work. Once that was sorted, I saw a lot of opportunities to contribute and make a difference in my job. I started enjoying my work every single day. One day I would be checking lentils and vegetables for their quality in massive stores that had bandicoots that scared big dogs away, and the very next day, I would be at the 'fresh point' wielding a large knife and cutting mutton and chicken carcasses to check for quality, wearing gloves and an apron over my sparkling, white, naval uniform.

To put it in a nutshell, the same organisation where I didn't want to work and received two warnings, sent my name for a commendation for excellence in work a couple of years down the line. That is what can happen when you work on your mindset. My work ethic and commitment were so appreciated that after two years there, I got another call from the same senior who had called me to check if I wanted to continue to stay in Mumbai. What he shared was music to my ears. They were looking for someone young and dynamic for their IT project.

My new appointment was to the Naval Pay Office, which was undertaking an ambitious IT project to re-develop the Naval Payroll system as the current system was not able to cope with the requirements. The project was given to an MNC, but they had thrown their hands up after about six months. They, and most outsiders don't have a clue about how complicated the Naval payroll system was (and still is). For example, two naval personnel of the same rank might get very different pay based on a number of parameters: their seniority, their additional qualifications, whether they were active in their qualifications, the city they were posted, and a hundred other things (maybe not a hundred, but there were too many permutations and combinations) to be checked before arriving at the pay due to them every month.

My dream was coming true. I was getting a chance to work on an actual software development project. I could not believe my ears or contain my excitement. That was another lesson for me. When I channelled my loyalty and excitement towards the opportunity I had in hand, my dreams and desires automatically manifested.

There was only one small issue. Even though I loved computers and was willing to spend any amount of time with it, I knew nothing about programming. I could not even write a simple loop function. While I was creating my software on board the ship during my watchkeeping before the accident, I had taken the help of a programming expert to write some loops and functions that made the program run smoothly. If you love to go on long drives, the easy part is buying the car. Once you have the car, you need to figure out how to drive it and that process is never an easy one.

Luckily, the Navy has answers to everything. I was to join the Naval Pay Office and then leave for an IT (Information Technology) managers' course that was to happen in (guess where) INS Hamla! This was a 7-month intensive course where programming was taught by C-DAC (Centre for Development of Advanced Computing) which was the premier R&D organisation of the Ministry of Electronics and Information Technology. Finally, I was back at INS Hamla.

The good thing about doing courses is that you are not disturbed by your organisation for any other work. You can really focus on the course (at least those who want to). Weekends used to be free from Saturday afternoon and as officers, we could do anything we wanted then. I used to spend time inside the base on Saturdays and on Sundays, I continued to go to church.

Now that I did not have to rush everywhere tending to the needs of my so-called fiancée, I realised that I had a lot of time at hand and that spending time with friends was a relaxing exercise. I had mentioned about Latha and Prakash, the brother-sister duo with whom I developed a very nice and deep bond of friendship. They lived in Shivaji Park, right next to the playground. Another thing that bonds Malayalis is the movies. Somehow, we always feel that non-Malayalis will never be able to understand and enjoy Malayalam films as much as we do. I guess it must be the same for all languages.

Since Malayali movie heroes were (times have changed now) not into body building, dancing, and martial arts (even though the original form or martial art, Kalaripayattu originated from Kerala), we could never do justice to any of those. Those few actors who did try most often ended up appearing clumsy or funny. I guess we were forced to focus on creating good story lines, excellent plots, and amazing acting. The result was that the Malayali community has made some really good movies in all genres.

After bonding with Latha and Prakash, my Sunday afternoons were spent at their home which included a sumptuous Malayali meal by Ammu, the duo's mother, followed by an afternoon movie in one of the Malayalam channels. It is a time that I always recall with a lot of happiness and fondness in my heart. They were totally selfless, all-loving and I was made part of their family from the first visit itself. We had similar tastes and I had someone to talk to in Malayalam after a long time. We used to discuss everything under the sun. From families and my breakup with the girl, to religion, especially the Bible since they were also born-again Christians from a very traditional Hindu family. We knew everything about our families and all-important relationships in our lives. I would leave very late in the evening back to my Officer's mess from there with a full tummy and happy mind. This became a weekly affair for me.

One day, while chilling at their home, I heard a very musical voice and to my utter surprise, saw Pallavi walk in. I later learned that she stayed very close to them and since she didn't have many friends in church, she had become close to my friends as well. I remember thinking, *well, this is crazy*. A few weeks ago, I was surprised to find her in the same mid-week church group which happened at Rajeev and Perola's home. They were the same couple who had helped me out of my previous situation. I was meeting Pallavi everywhere which was neither planned nor expected. It was as if she was being pushed in front of me everywhere by an invisible hand. We had become good friends by then, and I realised that beyond her drop-dead gorgeous looks, she was a very warm and fun-loving person who was very down to earth. I liked her a lot, but I still was very clear that I was not prepared to get into any kind of romance with a girl at this point.

But after a while, it became difficult to ignore the fact that she was present everywhere I went. It felt as though it was a sign from God that she was mine. Instead of being thrilled about it, I got into a fight with God in my prayers. *I didn't want to get into anything right now*, I reminded Him. Finally, I told Him that He had to show me for real if she was the one for me. I just did not want to make another mistake. I was deeply spiritual by then and I decided to let God handle this situation for me or at least give me clarity about the situation that I felt was cropping up in front of me. One of my constant prayers used to be 'Let thy will be done', especially after the painful experience of trying to have my way in life. I didn't want to be in any relationship, but I also didn't want to stop whatever was God's will to happen in my life. I finally went into fasting and praying for about 10 days by the end of which it was clear to me that she was meant for me. There was just one hitch. I don't think she had any inkling about it.

It's just not fair, is it? If she was meant for me, then some work had to be done there as well. It looked as though all the hard work was my responsibility.

One time, it was her birthday, and I was literally 'led' (read forced against my wish or my guts) to wish her, that too, at midnight. My friend, Harish had let me use his Tata Indica which was given to him by his sister (Lakshmi, my sister from my Pune family). I don't think I had ever been so scared about anything in my life before. I took the car out at about 2300h and drove to Matunga where she lived. I turned back twice along the way because my logical mind told me I was being stupid. However, I kept going and finally reached her place. I kept the cake on top of the car and called her out to wish her. I guess she was shocked beyond words but was courteous enough not to embarrass me and called me in to cut the cake. That was the first time I met her father and her mother (now Papa and Mama to me.)

Well, that didn't do much to change her mind. My first proposal was met with a very subtle *shakal-dekha-hai-kya*[32] kind of response. She didn't have to say it. Just the look was enough. Now that I knew she was the one, I didn't give up. She was a professional emcee for events and most of her events used to happen in the evenings, finishing late at night. My evenings were free, and I volunteered to accompany her to her events. It was amazing to see her in action.

---

[32] Local slang for saying 'Have you seen yourself' in a derogatory manner.

She was a very different person on stage. She was flawless in her speech, articulation, intonation and whatever else was associated with public speaking. Her looks and smile took her stage presence and delivery to a different level. She gave her everything on stage and naturally, by the end of it, used to be very tired and I was genuinely glad that I was there to drive her home after the events. She had bought a Maruti Zen with her earnings. I used to drop her back home, park the car, give her the car keys, and then walk to the local train station which was within walking distance from her home and take the local (many times the last local) to go back to Hamla, where I was doing my course.

Sundays became more interesting because Pallavi also joined us at Latha-Prakash's home. I didn't know that Pallavi used to watch Malayalam movies as a child when it used to be broadcasted on national television and she loved the story line (whatever she could understand). Now she had three people explaining the plot as well as the dialogue to her. In the evenings, all four of us used to go for a walk or eat out sometimes. Like many people from Mumbai, I fell in love with Tibbs Frankie during that time because that used to be one of our favourite spots.

Pallavi was everything that I was not. She was always cheerful, always had a smile and smiled at most people she saw (luckily, I didn't know this when she smiled at me for the first time. I thought she liked me and that's why she smiled). She could talk non-stop even with people she didn't know well and compared to her, I would come across as arrogant and constipated. Someone even told me this. That I come across as arrogant till they speak with me. Once they talk to me, they realise that I am very easy to talk to and some people even think that I am delightful (God bless them).

For some reason (I mean for all the right reasons), Pallavi's mom loved me from the instant she met me. I later found out that she kept hinting to Pallavi, much to her irritation, that Bimal was a very nice boy and would really take care of her. However, she somehow did not feel any 'chemistry' between us. I guess she had spent too much time in the media industry that she expected violins to play and rose petals to fall all around. While all that was not happening, she also realised along the way, as she got to know me better, that I was someone very solid and rooted and not the wavering and frivolous kind. Somehow, that began to grow on her.

One evening, she had done the launch of the Skechers brand in India and after the event, we drove back to her home. The event got finished early unlike some of her other events. We decided to stop at a nice spot. It was a small lane opposite Shivaji Park in Mumbai. It started from the main road and ended at the beach. I drove to the edge of the lane and stopped the car. The ambience of the moonlit night, soft music playing in the car stereo, her intoxicating perfume, and her presence next to me somehow gave me the courage to propose to her again. Maybe by then she realised that beyond violins and rose petals, I was someone who was going to be there, no matter what. Maybe I followed in the footsteps of Leonard in *Big Bang Theory*, and I wore her down albeit in a much shorter period (kudos to me). Whatever the case was, she smiled, and we kissed.

That night after dropping her home, I don't think I remember my travel back to Hamla because my heart was full, and my mind was totally occupied with my future life with Pallavi. I was ecstatic not just because she was too good to be true, but I knew deep in my spirit that she was the one. I had zero doubts regarding that. A certainty like that is a great help and support when you end up going through challenges in life, which invariably all couples go through. I informed my parents who were even happier to know that she wasn't a young girl, but a grown, mature woman. On top of everything, she was independent and doing very well in her media career as an emcee and voice-over artist with some of the top channels and as a TV host on some prestigious shows.

Her parents were also very happy. Her mom had accepted me as her son-in-law the very first time I met her. Her dad was also very happy to know that I was from the armed forces. Papa has a remarkable personality. After marriage, when we used to walk into the Naval Institute or the US club (United Services Club) for dinner, the sentry used to ignore me and salute Papa. Both Papa and Mama were idols and national heroes. Papa has been the coach for the Indian National Women's Hockey team for over 17 years. They really lived the movie 'Chak De' that too at a higher level. They both had built the Indian Railway Women's team from scratch. They went all over the country to scout for talent and brought the girls to Mumbai, and trained them to be great players. When there was a delay from the railways to give the girls accommodation, Papa and Mama happily accommodated all 16 girls in their one BHK railway quarters. He has two Padmashrees[33] and nine Arjuna Awardees[34] coached by him, who totally swear by him for all their achievements. Unfortunately, he has never received a Dronacharya[35] award despite being one of the most deserving coaches that Indian hockey has ever seen. Many of his juniors who assisted him went on to win the Dronacharya awards. I still feel that this is a huge injustice to Indian hockey itself. He was also a very respected international grade I umpire for many years.

I still had not asked Pallavi's dad for her hand in marriage. Her mom was quite religious, and we were going through a month where we were not supposed to discuss or decide good things as per the Hindu calendar. I was clearly not allowed to ask for her hand till

---

[33]Padma Shri (or Padma Shree) is the fourth-highest civilian award of the Republic of India conferred in recognition of 'distinguished contribution in various spheres of activity including the arts, education, industry, literature, science, acting, medicine, social service and public affairs'.
[34]The Arjuna Award, officially known as Arjuna Awards for Outstanding Performance in Sports and Games, is the second-highest sporting honour of India.
[35]The Dronacharya Award is for Outstanding Coaches in Sports and Games.

the month was over. I invited them over to stay at one of the beach shacks in Hamla for a weekend. They came over and were very happy to see the place and meet my friends. One day, while walking on the beach, her mom told me very sweetly, 'Son, we know you want to speak with us, but please wait for the month to get over.'

Well, the day the month was getting over, I was at her home with a close friend and coursemate, Pradeep, and his wife Nupur (*ladke wale*[36]) and as the clock struck 12, I was on a small stool next to her dad asking for Pallavi's hand in marriage. Since it was all known and accepted, he quietly listened to me and in the end hugged me, telling me to call him Papa from that day on. It was official!

Everything was set. It was not just a dream coming true. I also did not have any nagging thoughts or doubts that I could not explain, like the last time. She had just been selected to be the anchor for ESPN-Star Sports coverage of the ICC Cricket World Cup in South Africa. She had to be away for more than a month and I had to just wait for her to come back. It was agony. We decided that we would get married in August or September that year, 2003, so that we would get time to settle down. Me, in my new role at the Naval Pay Office as part of the project team as I was nearing completion of the course, and her, shifting out of her house to our new home at Colaba.

Everything was set and we were very happy that we were getting married soon. Pallavi left for South Africa with ESPN-Star Sports. I was sad that she was not around, but I was in for the treat of my life. Mama happens to be an amazing cook and once she learned that I love fish, there was no stopping her. Mama made dish after dish catering to every fish-eating desire of mine. I was the official son-in-law-to-be and they both cared for me like their own son. Since Pallavi was also away, I had all their attention. I was revelling in having the best time for my heart and tummy. But what is life without twists and turns, right?

---

[36]Hindi slag for groom's entourage

CHAPTER 10

UNCHARTED WATERS

Then came the next bombshell. I came to know that immediately after the course, I was being transferred to Visakhapatnam for my posting. It was shocking because I was sent for the IT course from the Naval Pay Office to train me to be part of the project. How could they now decide that I should be posted out of Mumbai? Mumbai indeed happens to be the most sought-after city for posting in the Indian Navy. A bustling city, with very active Naval life and loads of opportunities for spouses to get work. Therefore, most people, especially youngsters do not get to stay in Mumbai for long and I had already completed more than two years there, but I felt it was totally unfair and a waste of trained manpower. How could this happen just when everything was falling into place in my life after a long time?

I thought my world had ended (again). There was no way Pallavi was going to marry me if I moved to a city like Vizag. She was at the top of her career, working with the biggest names in media in the country. While Vizag had lovely beaches and scenery, when it came to her line of profession, it had nothing to offer. Besides, I had a personal disliking towards Vizag because of all the events that happened to me there. The only joyful memories that I had were with Raju and Payal but I was not in touch with them anymore. I just knew that Payal had joined the Airforce and Raju had moved to Hyderabad. Basically, I had nothing to look forward to in Vizag.

I realised that there was nothing much I could do about it as no one really could argue with the logic of 'service requirements' when it came to postings. It gives as much explanation as the computer error 'Bad command or Filename'. I begged and pleaded with Vivek sir who got me to the Naval Pay Office, and he said that he would try and do something if it was possible. The only challenge was that he was too junior in rank to be of any influence in matters like postings. I could not depend on that to rescue me, and I had to do what was honourable as a gentleman, as someone who had learned to really love someone, once again. I called Pallavi while she was in South Africa and gave her the news about my posting to Vizag and that there was nothing I could do about the posting. I also told her that there was no scope for any kind of media job in Vizag. With great difficulty, I told her that she didn't have to go with the marriage plans and that I would understand her if she wanted to call it off. She just heard me and cut the phone.

I was crestfallen. For once, I was sure that things were going in the right direction, and I could see a wonderful life ahead together for us and this spanner had to be thrown in, to screw things up. However, by then, I had this strange faith within me that if this was meant to happen, it would happen, and if not, I had to let it go without damaging myself or anyone else. I also had this prayer I depended on by then, 'God, if it is meant to be, make it happen. Else, you know better, and I am good with whatever you know is best for me.' Even today, I truly believe in this prayer because I know that if something is meant to be, it will happen and if not, there is something else waiting for me. There is no point in insisting and arguing with God that it had to be in a particular way and that it must be only that way. This small prayer, when said with full belief and conviction, liberates you. This has been my experience.

❊❊❊

I had learned this the hard way from my previous affair. There was a time midway through that affair when we had broken up for what felt like good. She had broken up with me for some reason that I can't even remember now. Anyway, once this happened, I was in a daily fight-and-beg mode with the Almighty to give her back to me as I felt then that she held the key to my everlasting happiness. I was so insistent that she came back into my life only to destroy it in a way that left me feeling worse than before. When I looked back after it was over, I could see that it was not meant to be and the indications were all there right from the start, but I ignored them. Finally, there had to be a divine intervention to get me out of it, but I was the idiot who would not see the truth. I was like a child whose favourite toy was yanked away because it was broken so that a new one could be given. The child in me had gotten so used to the toy, he could not see the value of a new, bigger and better toy, and so, insisted on the broken one.

By now, I knew that if something was being taken away from me, it just meant that it was not for me, and I just had to wait until I figured out the next steps. So, when the whole fiasco around the posting happened, I left the decision to Pallavi. Even though I was heartbroken, I was not just fine with my decision, but I was strangely peaceful about it.

Pallavi called me back as expected. She could not speak much then since she was in the middle of preparing for the next day's shoot. She asked me to explain the issue in detail as she could not understand everything fully the last time. I repeated everything and this time I was much calmer after the processing that I had gone through with myself. I told her about my unexpected transfer to Vizag, and that even though I had put in a request to cancel the transfer, there was nothing much I could really do about it. I also told her that Vizag was an industrial city, not the place where she could expect any kind of media presence.

'So?' she asked.

I once again explained that I would understand if she didn't want to go ahead with the plans as it could impact or even end her career.

She asked me, *'Hum sabzi lene ki baat kar rahe hai kya?'* (Are we talking about buying vegetables here?) She said she had decided to marry me and that it did not come with riders of me staying back in Mumbai. She shocked me out of my wits by suggesting that we should advance the wedding so that she could move with me to Vizag immediately after the course.

After the call, I just sat down trying to digest what she had just said. Women are strange. When they love, they love with everything they have. It's all about the heart for them. Such a situation would have put me in a great dilemma if our roles were reversed, but she didn't blink an eyelid before suggesting that we should get married earlier.

For me, it was like the clearing of storm clouds and clear skies being visible while sitting in a boat in the middle of the ocean. Everything changed once again. I was in a frenzy. The wedding that was supposed to happen after four or five months had to happen within the next two months. I was alone in Mumbai with no clue how to get things done. We had decided that we would not depend on our parents for money for our wedding and that we would sponsor the wedding ourselves.

As soon as I finished my course, I came back to the Naval Pay Office. Since I was under transfer to Vizag, I was asked to take over as the Assistant Secretary of the Officer's Institute that was next to the Western Naval Command Officer's mess. The Officer's Institute was always a happening place. Situated right next to the sea, it is a beautiful place filled with activities for officers and their families and in the evening, the entire place transforms into a lovely restaurant with really good food. The ambience was unmatched because there was outdoor sitting, and some tables would be right next to the railing that overlooked the Arabian sea. The place also had different kinds of entertainment all through the week ranging from tambolas[37], movie nights, match nights and many more. It's a great place to experience the very best of naval life but when you are on the other side, you don't get to enjoy it so much because everything had to be arranged by the Secretary and his assistant. This was a place frequented by senior officers and their spouses. This was also the hub of activities and get-togethers for NWWA (Naval Wives' Welfare Organisation). The fact that my secretary chose to take leave during that time did not help me at all. There were also a couple of visits by Flag Officers.

All through the day, I was busy with work. After work, I had to plan for the wedding. Luckily by then, Pallavi was back, and we got right down to it together. There was just one little detail we had not catered for. We were supposed to get engaged prior to the wedding.

We had to work simultaneously on our wedding as well as our engagement now. From the design and colour of the wedding card to the venue for the nuptials, the venue for the reception after

---

[37]The game of Housie

the nuptials, the table arrangements, the menu, sweet dishes, the wedding gown, the wedding cake, my uniform for the nuptials and suit for the reception, list of invitees, inviting people and sending the cards to people who were out of station... Phew! Every single detail had to be considered and decided by just the two of us. We decided to get engaged on the institute lawns itself with only our families.

While I was making the list of invitees, the only people I had listed down for my engagement were my parents, my cousins who were family to me, and my Pune family. Even my coursemates were not invited to our engagement. I had no option but to invite my parents and my cousins over a phone call as they were in Kerala but I was clear that I would not invite Amma and Lak (my Pune family) via phone call for my engagement and wedding. I took out the card that was written for them and kept it separate so that I could go to Pune along with Pallavi and invite them in person for the engagement and wedding. They had become everything to me over the last nine years. They were my family; their home was my home. We had been through thick and thin together.

Harish had lost his father while we both were in Pune on a weekend. That Sunday morning, Lak frantically called out to both of us who were sleeping in the front room that their dad was not responding. We rushed to him, and I started rubbing his feet to warm them. And then I felt it. His legs suddenly went stiff and then they went limp. I can never forget that in my entire life. I knew he was gone and there was nothing I could do. We survived that, our bonds grew stronger and then Lak met her wonderful husband, Vijay, got married and she was happy. I had not just been a witness to everything in their lives, I was an integral part of every joy, every sorrow, every celebration, all through the past nine years. There was no decision taken in their household without discussing it with me as well. They had become closer than my own family. Lak and Amma were always there for me. When I graduated as an officer one year later, my parents could not reach for the ceremony, but Lak was there. Even when Harish moved out to do his specialization courses, I was always there instead of him, and Lak was always there instead of my sisters. I had become very protective of Lak as though she was my own younger sister even though she was older than me. Given how close we were, the only way I could invite them was by visiting them in person with Pallavi, and spending a day with them during one of the weekends. I really wanted Pallavi to see and understand what they meant to me.

I realised the importance of wedding planners during this phase of my life. The biggest advantage is that you can actually be 'present' during your own engagement. In my case, I was running the Officer's Institute singlehandedly and the engagement and wedding preparations with the help of Pallavi. It was so chaotic that my mind was entirely occupied throughout the engagement. Pallavi told me many times to relax and enjoy the process, but I couldn't. And the reason was not the arrangements. At the engagement party, as I saw my parents and cousin walk towards the venue, I felt a chill go down my spine all the way to my feet and I got that sinking feeling into the depths of my soul. I could not find Lak and *Amma* in the crowd because I had forgotten to invite them!

I wanted to cry but I couldn't. None of these people knew what they meant to me. How in the world could I forget? Since I was planning to go to Pune and invite them, obviously, I did not send them my card by post. Therefore, I had not only forgotten to invite them, but I had also not even sent them a courtesy wedding card to inform them.

I just could not get my head around this. I always teach people that finding time is about having priorities. You will always find the time to do something that is truly important to you. I did not have an explanation for what had just happened. I still don't. I still cannot freaking understand how I forgot to invite the two most important people in my life after my biological family. I was filled with guilt and shame. I still am. I could not find a logical explanation for what had happened. How could I face them? What would I tell them? How could I explain this to them?

I just could not find an answer and in that depth of despair, shame, and guilt, I did the next worst thing possible. I did not have the courage to go to them and ask for forgiveness. I was too chicken, too scared, too hurt, and unforgiving of myself that I did not rectify one of the biggest regrets of my life. I ran away from their lives hoping that I never have to face them again. Even now I long to be in touch with them, to know how Lak is doing, but it has reduced to just a courtesy enquiry about her with Harish, that too once in a blue moon. I still get very emotional and feel extremely guilty about what happened. I have had countless conversations with Lak and *Amma* in my head asking them for forgiveness but to date, even though I have her number and email, I have not been able to express myself. I guess I must forgive myself first to be able to ask the same from them. I am yet to figure out how to do that…

The very next month, our wedding was planned. One of the toughest things to happen when you get posted to Mumbai is getting a house in Navy Nagar. The normal waiting period at that time was about 18 months. There was one silver lining, though. To encourage officers to get married late, there was a rule that anyone who was getting married after 25 years, half of the period from the 25th birthday to the marriage date would be given as seniority to be considered for flat allotment. I was nearing 30 at that time and I realised that I could get 'walk-in' accommodation, meaning I wouldn't have to wait at all.

We were to leave for Kerala the day after our marriage. I wanted Pallavi to walk into a proper home immediately after marriage. Therefore, we decided to register our marriage with the registrar a few days after the engagement so that we could have our home by the time we had our official wedding. We did that and as expected, I got the house allotted a week before the official wedding. That one week went in getting furniture for the house and finally, I had just enough time to dump my stuff from the officers' mess to my new house. I remember drawing a couple of circles with cockroach killer chalk around all my belongings that were literally dumped in the middle of the drawing room before rushing out for my wedding.

When Pallavi came into my life, she brought all good things along with her. To start with, once I reached Kerala, where we were staying for a week, I received a call from my senior Vivek sir who informed me that my Vizag posting has been cancelled and I was retained at Naval Pay Office for at least a year. My joy knew no bounds. Pallavi was truly my Lady Luck, and I knew things were going to change for the better, now that she was in my life.

As soon as I reached back to the office, I was put directly into the project team. I now think that if I was part of the project, instead of being a secretary during my wedding, I may not even have got a week's leave because my wedding happened during the thick of the IT project. It was an ambitious project by the Navy. The MNC, as mentioned earlier, had decided that the project was not viable for the amount they had quoted, and they put their hands up. After it got dumped by them, it also became a prestige issue for the Navy to make it work. So, in the best of Naval traditions, they put together a team of officers and men who had some idea about coding and project management and asked them to deliver the finished work. The team was not big. We had fewer than ten officers and around ten men working on the project.

Luckily, we had Ramki, who was a whiz with computers, and he did what he could to make things happen. Even though he was a junior, there was a lot of respect for his talent in the team and he expertly guided the team in the very complex technicalities. When compared to the IT experience of the team, which was literally zero, this came in handy.

Pallavi and I were very happy with the house that got allotted and everything else was fine too, but what was challenging was my office timings. We were working frantically for the project to happen as per the timeline and the fact that I was newly married did not matter much to the project. I used to leave home before 9 AM and I used to get back well past 9 PM. This happened every single day, including Saturdays, which were only slightly better. Pallavi had to wait the whole day all alone in the house. We had decided not to have a television at home and for a very long time, we did not have one. She had to figure out how to pass her time. She grew up in the bustling part of Mumbai and NOFRA (Naval Officers Family Residential Area) was just the opposite. It looks and feels nothing like traditional Mumbai. We could hear birds throughout the day there. Pallavi was a freelancer, and her work was not a daily affair. She was growing restless due to my unavailability for long periods during the days and now, whatever work she got was very far from NOFRA, which was right at the edge of Mumbai. The only thing beyond NOFRA was the Arabian Sea.

Due to my extended working hours, I started losing out on socialising as well. There was no time during the weekdays, and during weekends, we would go to Pallavi's home to visit her parents.

On some weekends, they used to come over. During this time, I was doing so much coding with Oracle that I decided to become an Oracle-certified professional. I bought lots of books, but the only time I could study was when I was home after work. This meant that I was even less available to Pallavi. I had decided that since my medical category would never get upgraded, I should leave the service and plunge into corporate life. The best way to do it was to pass my CAT exam and then somehow resign from the Navy and pursue my dreams. New dreams, I should say.

Since my availability was reducing and we could not do much about it, we realised that the only thing we could do was to enjoy whatever little time we had together instead of sulking or fighting about it. Pallavi also decided to focus more on her work.

Having Pallavi in my life changed my life completely. I have always been a recluse and more of an introvert, and she was just the opposite. Her energy was (and still is) very infectious and that is the first thing everyone notices about her. Due to her profession, I started attending corporate events, award functions, Bollywood events, and fashion shows. Whenever she had an evening event, I went after my work to meet her there and we would come back together. I met all the Bollywood stars, including Big B[38], because of her. She participated in Gladrags[39] Mrs India and won the first runner-up and best model titles. She also landed a job to be a visiting professor with the SP Jain Institute of Management in Dubai, Singapore and Mumbai, because of which I did my first international trip to Dubai. She also covered the Milan Fashion Week in Italy and visited all the lovely places there. Even though I

---

[38] Amitabh Bachchan (also known as Big B) is an Indian actor, film producer, television host, occasional playback singer and former politician who is regarded as one of the most successful and influential actors in the history of Indian cinema.

[39] Gladrags is an Indian magazine, published biweekly featuring modeling and related events

could not accompany her on that trip, life was always exciting with her around.

The challenge in achieving a lot of things early in life is that you need more challenging things to work for, to aspire for. I had read somewhere that the astronauts who went to the moon went into depression after they came back. After achieving such a lofty goal, how do you raise the bar?

Something similar started happening to Pallavi. She, for some unfathomable reason, started losing interest in work, started avoiding calls for work, and would just sit at home and do nothing. She was someone who had started working and earning from the age of 16, and she was getting quite frustrated with herself now, something she could not explain. I was also getting a little worried about her. During one of those days, she got a call from one of her close friends, Srikant, who was also a guide and advisor to her. We were called over for lunch at their place in Mumbai. We were very happy to go over for the Parsi lunch. Little did we know that our lives were going to change forever.

I was to meet them for the first time that day. I had only heard about Srikant from Pallavi. He was into motor sporting events, especially the off-roading ones (my favourite type). He was in the Limca Book of Records for something related to events. I was a fan even before we reached their home. We were welcomed by a fine gentleman in his 50s. He was greying, wore spectacles, and had a very friendly demeanour. His wife was very sweet. They welcomed us into their home which was on the top floor of a building that overlooked the beautiful Marine Drive. It was a sight to behold.

They were very easy to talk to and Pallavi, being a natural talker, helped in keeping the conversation alive. He offered us wine, and we had a great time together. Once it was lunchtime, we were invited to a delightfully delicious Dhansak[40] which was their signature dish. It was the first time I had it, and I loved it. The lunch was followed by some amazing handmade ice cream, something difficult to find. They have a very different taste than all the machine-made ones.

As an afterthought, he shared that he had gotten started with a new business opportunity and he was looking for partners to work with him. I was more than willing to have a look at anything that might interest Pallavi to get her back into action mode. He was new to the whole business idea, and he had some printouts with some circles drawn on it. I saw it and my heart sank. It looked like a network marketing business. I had no idea about MLM[41], but I knew that I would never get associated with something that even remotely resembled MLM. I only knew these as scams and a business where you force friends and family into it. Something that I surely did not want to get associated with.

However, Pallavi had never even heard of this word or the industry. For her, everything was new. The kind of returns that were shown in the plan, even through a lazy man's projection (A projection of results even if you do the business at a snail's pace), were mind-blowing. There is a saying that if something is too good to be true, it probably is. I switched off somewhere along the way but could not deny the logic behind the whole plan and presentation. One thing that really struck me was the fact that considering what we were doing in our lives currently, we would never reach the numbers shown in this plan, even if we worked our whole life. I remained cynical about the whole thing.

On the other hand, Pallavi was ecstatic about the plan and projections. It looked very easy and doable for her. After she saw the

---

[40]**Dhansak** is a popular Indian dish, originating among the Parsi Zoroastrian community. It combines elements of Persian and Gujarati cuisine.
[41]Multi-Level Marketing

plan, we sat together, and she was brimming with excitement. She said she had a very good feeling about it and that she wanted to do it and wanted my full support. All husbands know one fundamental truth about our wives asking for our suggestions or input. Even when they ask us to help them choose between two dresses, the truth is that they would have already made their minds up about which dress to wear and are only looking for validation of their choice. If we choose the wrong one by chance, they will want to know why not the other one (the one they had decided on). They will start asking a lot of questions as to why we chose the dress we did. Husbands! Nod your head if you agree.

When it came to this MLM business, I did not have to think much. Her excitement won over my cynicism about the industry, and I thought it would give her something to be interested in and be occupied with. I had told her clearly that I would not be able to be part of it for multiple reasons. My work hours, my lack of belief in that industry, and so on. However, I assured her of all backend support that she might require to go ahead.

One thing that stands out about Pallavi is her belief and optimism. Whenever something is presented to her, she sees the possibilities and I see the challenges. We are like the accelerator and brake of a sports car. According to me, just having the option of an accelerator is a sure recipe for disaster and only the brakes can ensure that the car doesn't even move forward.

Together we brought balance to every situation.

However, in this case, her enthusiasm won me over. She was a dream prospect for any networker. In Network Marketing, once we finish presenting the business plan, we must wait for the prospect/guest to speak. It is always an awkward pause while he/she ponders over to make his/her decision. Normally, when some of them consider starting with the lowest possible investment (buy a product/service), they are informed with the advantages of starting with a larger investment to increase their financial commitment to the business. It not only increases the chances of better returns; it also makes sure that they put efforts into the business. I have seen too many people come into the business with a let-me-try attitude and then give up before speaking to even three people. That happens only because the money they put in was negligible, unlike starting a traditional business.

In the case of Pallavi, she could only see the big possibilities. She went in with the highest possible entry at the time. She also brought in her parents. The expectation wasn't that they would work the business, but it was a smart move because if our parents were immediately after us, they would also get the benefits of all that we would do. She was so excited that it seemed to scare Srikant's wife. She told Pallavi multiple times that she could start with a lower spend instead of putting everything she had into it, but Pallavi just would not listen. Her credit card did not have the required limit. Srikant had to use his credit card and we assured him that we would repay the amount in the next couple of days.

We left only by late evening, and we were ecstatic about the possibilities that Pallavi saw. The possibilities that suddenly opened for her and our future seemed too good to be true. The logic for doing the business was irrefutable. It was all about leveraging everyone's time and effort where everyone benefited from the effort. I realised that I didn't need to demean any industry, provided it was legal, ethical, and moral to do the business, and we were very sure that our friend would never get us into anything illegal. He was doing very well for himself and more than that, the reputation that he had built over decades was at stake. We felt very confident about our decision as well as how it was going to change our lives.

We reached home. I decided to do some research about what Srikant shared with us (and we were already a part of). I have this habit where if I am to do something, I must know everything about it. I can spend days and nights deep-diving and finding everything I can about it. I came home and started doing some research online about the company and its products. It was a relatively new company and did not have lots of information online, but I did not give up.

Then I saw what I feared. One article that clearly stated that the company and their business model were a scam. My heartbeat quickened, and I opened the article. There were long explanations as to why the company, the products and the whole plan were devised only to scam people off their money and how no one ever made any money in this business. I had to share the news with Pallavi. She read it and broke down.

We realised that in our excitement we didn't do our due diligence before investing, we didn't consult with anyone about this, neither her parents nor mine, and on top of it all, she had spent money for her parents also to be part of the business. We could not fathom how Srikant could do something like this to us. It was too late at night to call him and ask. We just sent a text saying that we would like to meet him the next evening. We were crestfallen. Everything was looking upbeat just a couple of hours ago and now, it felt as though it was just an air bubble and it burst in our faces. Pallavi cried herself to sleep that night. I confess I had a lot of difficulty falling asleep as well.

The next morning was bright outside, but we had a dark cloud looming over our heads. We somehow spent the day focusing on other things and in the evening, we drove to his home hoping that he would be kind enough to help us get out of this mess and get our money back. We sat down in his living room, and I shared what I had read online about the company and the plan. To my surprise, he let out a hearty and loud laugh and said, 'Oh, you also have seen that article?'

I was confused. Why would he be part of something if he also knew it was a scam? He assured me that everything was in order and that we did not have to worry about anything. The only thing he requested was that we should attend the weekly training that happened in Bandra. Bandra wasn't very close to where we lived, and we had to reach there by 1900 h sharp, which itself was quite a task in the always-deadlocked Mumbai. We reluctantly agreed to his request and felt confident that if he was aware of the article and was still confident about it, he must have a solid reason for it. We thanked him and, on our way out, he handed us some CDs that had training modules and gave us a sheet of paper with a list of books to read and understand about the industry. We accepted both and left his place.

Once we were home, I started watching a couple of CDs. The speakers were from the company, and I felt like they were genuine people. Either they were genuine, or they were very well-trained to come across as that genuine. The CD explained a lot of how the business model could change lives, how it changed the speaker's life, and the whole spiel. I was quite motivated by what the speaker shared.

The following Wednesday, we went for the training as scheduled and Srikant was there to make sure we were at the right place. He introduced us to a couple of people there. I think that was the last time we saw him in the context of the business he introduced us to. They are very sweet people, and I will always be grateful to them because they changed our lives forever with that informal business meeting over Dhansak and wine.

What I saw at the training was something I can never forget. I saw many people from various walks of life at the meeting. I could see professionals, businessmen, investment bankers and CXOs of reputed companies sitting with us in the meeting. The kind of people who were involved in the business gave me the confidence that all these people collectively could not have been duped and made fools of by anyone. We were inexperienced, but the collective knowledge and experience in the room were good enough to test and audit any business plan. The meeting immediately helped bring our belief in the business back to where it was initially. The possibilities began to dance in front of us again. We were sure that we would be millionaires in a few years. Pallavi, with her typical enthusiasm, called her enterprising cousin, Rupa, who was in Bangalore and told her that she was going to 'change her life' and took the next flight out to Bangalore.

Something else happened while Pallavi was away in Bangalore. I have this burning need for clarity in whatever I do. It is difficult for me to operate in grey areas where things are not very clear to me. For me, the industry of network marketing was in that space, all grey and unclear. I had heard of a lot of people losing money and getting cheated out of their savings, and at the same time, the kind of people I had met did not seem to be the 'duping' kind of people. Since I had this conflict in mind, I decided to get more clarity on this. Not for anything else but for my understanding.

The printout that Srikant gave had the names of six books that were 'recommended' by the team. I had never heard of any of these books or the authors. I went to the famous 'fountain' area of Mumbai. In those days, the footpaths there used to be full of vendors selling used books.

I did not have the patience to search for these books, so I called one youngster who was handling one of the 'shops'. I gave him the list and asked him to get me all the books. Surprisingly, he found all six books and brought them to me in about 15 minutes. Most of them were in good shape and reasonably priced since this was not one of those industries that were popular. I looked at all the books and decided to start with a book written by Mr Robert Kiyosaki.

❋❋❋

I guess I can call that one of the defining moments of my life. I have always been a voracious reader, but always been into fiction. This was the first non-fiction book that I picked up to read and soon I became a big believer in making people read books, especially about things that they have reservations about. I had these objections towards the industry based on assumptions which maybe had no factual basis. Many times, we tend to have reservations and form opinions towards a person/industry/product based on hearsay and that too from people who have no real experience with the person/industry/product. When we do not have any foundational facts or statistical data, we tend to hold on to our opinions vehemently and we argue our case emotionally, not factually. The challenge with emotional objections is that we tend to fight more even though we don't have grounds for a level-headed argument. This is where a book comes in.

You can't argue with a book. When you cannot argue with a book, you end up reading more to get more information and at some point, if it starts to make sense, your brain ends up telling you, 'What this guy says rings true.' That is exactly what happened to me. The more I read, the more I was convinced about the principles and practices of this industry and by the end of book one, I was a fan. I knew I was in the right place. Eagerly, I read the rest of the pile as well. At the end of her week in Bangalore, Pallavi walked back into the house dejected and declared that she would never make another presentation ever again in her life. But by then, I had become a crusader for the industry.

One of the biggest things the industry did for me was that it opened me up to the world of personal development. Way back in 2006, it was unheard of in India. Luckily, the people I was involved with as well as the company believed in developing people in a big way. For the first time in my life, I learned that I could achieve more than what I had thought was possible for me. I was mesmerised by the sheer power that washed over me, knowing that I could craft a different life than the one I felt I was destined for. It was like discovering the hidden world of Atlantis.

With that enthusiasm, backed by a factual understanding of the industry, we both started connecting with people to see if anyone wanted to have a look at what we were doing. A few weeks into the business, we received a cheque for a very small amount as a commission for Pallavi's decision to sign up her parents. I still remember how we jumped with joy. Suddenly all the things that we had seen on paper became real to us. It didn't matter that the amount was very small because if we could get a small commission for generating small revenue for the company, all we had to do was to talk to more people and make sure that more products were bought, generating higher revenue for the company and commissions for us. This information was life-changing. There was no limit to what we could achieve through this business.

People say network marketing is easy money. Nothing could be farther from the truth. This is one of the toughest industries, but the rewards outweigh the efforts. After a point, more than the money, it's the difference that you make to other people's lives that keeps you going. This is the best example of Zig Ziglar's quote: '*If you help enough people pay their bills, your bills automatically disappear.*'

We were meeting so many different kinds of people. From professionals to businessmen, from home-makers to CEOs and CXOs of Fortune 500 companies, from artists to musicians. Every meeting was interesting. Every conversation was inspiring. I learned so much about various industries, businesses, work cultures, family issues, people's dreams and aspirations, and things that inspire them as well as stop them. I found all of it riveting, to say the least. There was never a dull moment for me.

Two specific people helped us take the business to the next level. One was my senior, Cdr Dhillon, in the Indian Navy. His wife also decided to join us in the business. We were in the same office and in the same team. He had just taken over as my HOD at the Naval Pay Office. He is one of those rare people who can fiercely focus on the project work all day long and then focus on the business with equal ferocity once the working hours were over. We were very clear that we wouldn't talk to each other about business and would be 100% focused and committed towards office work during the day and if we had to build the business, then it would have to be during our personal time after working hours. This was a pact that we honoured all through the journey.

The second was my childhood friend Krishnakumar, Kikkan to me (I have already told you about him in the first chapter), who was then working in a top corporate firm in Bangalore. When Pallavi had gone to meet her cousin there, I had asked her to meet him as well. Though he did meet with Pallavi and saw the business plan, he did not show much interest in it. Later, I had to go to Kerala for a short visit and Kikkan was also there on leave. I explained more about the business to him, but he did not make any commitment and told me that he would let me know his decision when I visit him in Bangalore since my return was already planned via Bangalore. After he left Kerala, I focused on the primary reason I was there. Just the way Pallavi wanted to change the life of her cousin in Bangalore, I too wanted to do the same for all my childhood friends.

I called my friends for dinner and gathered them around a table at a restaurant and with all excitement, shared the plan with them. I did not doubt that they would all come into the fold. To my shock and horror, they literally laughed at me for doing this illogical business. I was hurt and upset. I was getting rejected by the people I had counted on the most for support in my new business. In that hurt and rage, I challenged them and told them that I would prove to them that it would work. They challenged me back asking me to prove it by earning a huge amount of money every month in two years. We agreed on the amount, and I wrote it down with the current date and the target date on the same sheets on which I was sharing the plan.

I was crestfallen by the time I left Kerala for Bangalore. Even Kikkan had not given any kind of positive response before he left. Since I was staying with him, once I reached his home, out of courtesy, I asked him if he did think about the business at all. I still remember his reply because it was music to my ears. He said, '*Machu*[42], let's do it.'

I was over the moon, and I got him signed up then and there.

That is one of the amazing things about this industry. Even if you go through 100 rejections and feel low, when one person decides to partner with you, the whole scenario changes because that one person could be responsible for changing the entire growth

---

[42]Malayalam slang meaning brother

trajectory of your business. That is exactly what happened with Kikkan. He shared this with one of his close friends who took up the business in a big way. Our team started growing very fast, both in Mumbai and Bangalore. Pallavi and I decided to split efforts so that Pallavi could handle the Bangalore team and I could handle the Mumbai one.

I always had the sheet where the challenge with my childhood friends was written. I used to look at that sheet very often and it motivated me further to do the business. After two years, I had the privilege of calling all my friends to the same restaurant for dinner to announce to them, as I showed them the sheets, that I had achieved the target almost a year back. With these guys, it was never about bragging or being mean. It was more of a statement about my ability and my belief in the business. They were also very happy to see my growth and the fact that I had achieved the milestone early. We celebrated my win that night.

❊❊❊

I had shared how this industry also opened the world of personal development for me. Unfortunately, personal development does not necessarily mean financial education or financial intelligence. Schools and colleges don't teach anything about managing and growing money. No one had taught us about investing and growing our money so that at one point our money would start working for us. Thanks to our hard work and the work of the team, our income grew multifold and soon we didn't have to worry about money at all. The reason why most lottery winners lose all their money is due to a lack of financial knowledge and ability to manage their money. We were no different initially. We were just enjoying the short-term pleasures of life and were more focused on spending it and enjoying life instead of investing it in the right places. The knowledge that we were getting another commission cheque the next week made us splurge our hard-earned money. When everything is going fine, we feel invincible, especially when it happens for the first time in our lives.

Close to a year into the business, the company went through a challenge. Challenges happen with all businesses, and this was no different. Some people were doing the business unethically and there were negative reviews and news online. I remembered how we had felt after seeing one article online before we started, and I knew what was going to happen this time as well. Suddenly, the outpouring of money was reduced to a trickle. I woke up from the comfortable daze that I was in. I knew that we had earned a lot of money by then, but I could not find any trace of it in the bank accounts. I decided to take stock and went into the 'commissions earned' section on the virtual office and I froze. I had to recheck it to make sure I was seeing things right. We did have money in the bank account, but it was nothing compared to what we had earned. We had been spending money like there was no tomorrow. I sat down with Pallavi and gave her the news. We were scared to tell our parents because we were pretty sure about how they would react. We took a decision that we need to start saving and investing our money.

We were still clueless about managing finances. I came from a middle-class family where money was just enough to make ends meet. My father was into real estate, and he had been hounding me to buy real estate in Kerala. I was not very interested in it because I felt that I would never settle down in Kerala. The whole idea of buying property as an investment never occurred to me. We decided to buy a flat in Mumbai and we saw some which were in decent locations and were affordable. We had this thing fixated on our minds that we should buy a flat only if we would stay in it and most of the flats did not live up to that because even though the Naval homes were big and spacious, the normal homes in Mumbai were not.

Today, I realise the importance of financial education at an early age for my child, and in fact, for all children. It was just my mindset that prevented me from investing in all the opportunities that came our way.

We finally decided that we would not look at properties for now (which was a really bad decision) and focus on saving and investing the money where it can grow much faster. Once it reached a critical point, then we could think of other things. Other opinions were also floating around that stopped us from investing in property at that time. One was about my job being a transferrable one and that I may not be able to take care of my property once I move out of Mumbai. Another was the thought process that buying a property was not a great decision as it would be blocking my capital and the opportunity cost would be huge if the property value does not appreciate, among many other fears.

Finally, we dropped the idea of buying a property in Mumbai or Pune and ended up buying a piece of land in Kerala with the help of my father.

Mumbai is a dream posting for anyone in the Navy. Officers are never given a Mumbai tenure for more than three years normally and in rare cases, five years. I had been in Mumbai for seven years. Transfers are taken care of by the Department of Personnel in Naval Headquarters, New Delhi, and we used to joke that their system would be throwing alerts and alarms every time about my tenure in Mumbai.

As luck would have it, I got an offer to get posted to the Naval Headquarters in New Delhi. This was exactly what I wanted. I had decided that I would leave the Navy as there was not much scope for me concerning promotions because of my low medical category. Also, I had no control over where I would get posted during my career. Our teams in our business were growing quickly and they needed our help and guidance. Once I realised that there was more to life than getting a better-paying corporate job and that I could never create wealth as an employee, I happily shelved my dream of attempting the CAT exam and going to a management school. I was already creating wealth and was financially free. I needed to focus on this and make sure that I was available to our teams to help them grow. A transfer to the NHQ (Naval Headquarters) meant that when I put in my papers to leave service, it would go directly to the decision-maker and the Department of Personnel, and the chances would be much higher for it to get approved.

The cherry on the cake was that, by now, we knew the potential of the business we were part of and we had built a solid team. We knew how amazing our lives were going to be in the next few years.

CHAPTER 11

BETTER TO LIGHT THE CANDLE

Just when we thought that we had it all, our worlds turned upside down, both Pallavi's and mine. Pallavi was sobbing on my shoulder. This cannot be true, right? Please tell me this is not true…. I had gone numb. For a while, I didn't know what was happening around me. I thought the world and everything around me were caving in right at that moment. This just could not be true. We had spent the last eight years slogging every single day of our lives. We had sacrificed our personal lives for a better tomorrow. It was our sweat, tears, long hours, sleepless nights. We even lived separately in different cities to build our business. We lived frugally to build our wealth. Now, all that toil seemed wasted. Just when all the hard work was about to bear fruit, just when we were slowing down to really have a life, spend time together and travel the world. We were dollar millionaires a day before and now we were left with what we had in our savings accounts.

When I regained my composure, I realised that it wasn't a bad dream. We were sitting in one of our friend's houses with a few other people, all of them looking deeply concerned and scared. It is not every day that we come to know that our entire life's savings have been wiped out by someone whom we trusted completely. How could Dhanunjay do this to us? He has always been a gentleman. He was introduced to us by Maloni, one of our closest friends. Over a period, Dhanunjay had become a good friend to us.

He had come all the way to Pune from Mumbai to meet Pallavi's parents, and had shared a meal with us. Dhanunjay has been our investment advisor and manager for the past three years. He had given us excellent advice and returns. He gave us documents of our investments and assured us of a good, retired life by the time I turned 40 years old. Pallavi's parents have always been a big support to us, and we wanted them also to take advantage of the better returns that he was giving. They had never invested in anything other than FDs and Post Office. Dhanunjay volunteered to come to Pune with us so that he could talk to them and give them his assurance and support. He had helped us with timely returns from our investments all this while. With his assurances and promises, even Pallavi's parents agreed to move their FDs, retirement benefits and savings to his investments. That was one of our biggest mistakes. The year was 2013.

●●●

Leaving Naval Pay Office was not easy for me. It was one of the most fulfilling tenures of my life. I got married there, I got to fulfil my dream of working with computers and I worked on two live projects that were very complicated. I was part of the core team for developing the complex payroll for the Navy, which is still running today. Later, I was picked for another major IT project that was like an extension to the payroll system.

This was a very complex, two-part system, where one part had to be implemented in more than 300 ships and units across the

Navy. I came to know later that there were two earlier attempts to get this done but both had failed. The second part was even more complex where the two independent systems had to be linked. To cut the long story short, I accomplished it with the help of a two-man team, and I was awarded the commendation from the Chief of Naval Staff for exceptional professional work going beyond the call of duty. One of the proudest moments of my life to date.

All this happened simultaneously while building teams in our part-time business. There was never a time when I was not working. But this only made me much more productive and focused. I knew I had limited time to work the job and the business. My focus became laser sharp.

This was the time my transfer to NHQ (Naval Headquarters) had come through. I had to report there in June 2007. I had been to New Delhi a couple of times as my sisters were working there, but never really lived there for a long period. There are always mixed reactions about Delhi, especially from those who lived in Mumbai.

I received multiple opinions about Delhi, especially about the harsh weather, the traffic, and the people in general. I had been into various personal development training as part of the business and one thing I learned from watching the movie *The Secret* was that we normally get what we really expect. I decided that I liked Delhi even before I left Mumbai. I think it is like falling in love. When you love someone, you tend to see the good things about that person. The same things apply to places also, I guess. Since I had already decided that I liked Delhi, when I reached there, I could see the nice and wide roads, open spaces, gardens, parks and all the places I could visit in and around the city.

It was peak summer in Delhi when I landed, and I got temporary accommodation at the Officer's Institute for a couple of months till I was allotted a house. Since I was allowed to retain my Mumbai house for a few more months, Pallavi decided to stay back and visit me once a month. My commute was on my Honda (Activa, actually) and since Google maps did not exist at that time, I had to chalk out my route first on the paper map even to places like Noida and Faridabad and then ride there. I realised that Delhi roads were not very safe as many times I had to return after meetings late at night and my Activa was either too insignificant or invisible to the multitude of interstate trucks that plied on the roads at high speeds.

I decided to apply another principle that I had learnt from my trainings as well as the movie *The Secret*. It was about writing down my goals and dreams. My morning routine was set, and I would get up in the morning and the first thing I would do was write down my goals and dreams. There was one interesting goal that I started writing after I reached Delhi. It was buying a new Scorpio.

While I was at the Naval Pay Office, we had embarked on a vehicle safari across Rajasthan and had vehicles sponsored by Tata and Mahindra. I got a chance to drive the Scorpio extensively during this trip and fell in love with it. I liked it so much that Pallavi and I even took a test drive. But we could not afford it then since it was way before we started doing the business. Now that finance was not an issue, I thought of revisiting that dream and I started writing about it every day. However, I had not mentioned this to Pallavi and after the test drive a few years back, we had not really discussed buying another car.

It is true that when we start writing our goals and dreams, they do manifest. Mine too happened most unexpectedly. Pallavi decided to visit me in July, which was still peak summer. I borrowed a Maruti 800 from a friend of mine. The car did not even have an

AC. I picked up Pallavi from the airport and got her to the institute and as I was parking the car, she blurted out, 'Beems, I really think you should buy the Scorpio immediately.'

I was speechless for a moment and then I shared with her how I was writing it from the time I reached Delhi. It was like a confirmation. Things happened quickly after that. I booked the car through the Naval Canteen, and took the delivery at Chandigarh even though my agent had told me that he would get the car to my doorstep. I wanted to go through the whole experience of taking delivery of the car and driving it all the way to Delhi. When you have a dream car and when you drive it for the first time, the experience and the joy are inexplicable. I enjoyed every moment of that 5-hour drive back to Delhi.

Everything was happening wonderfully well. I started growing a team in Delhi, I had my accommodation. Pallavi shifted in with me and we had the biggest of our joys, our blessing, our Giaa-Marie. Life couldn't be better.

After we went through the jolt of figuring out that we had wasted most of the money we earned initially, we took a conscious decision to save money and invest it in such a way that we could retire financially by the time I turned 40. We decided to dedicate our lives to this goal. Luckily by then, my request to be allowed to leave service on compassionate grounds got approved. This meant that I could build my business full-time and take it to a totally different level.

I had spent a total of 17 years in the armed forces. It made me who I was. I am and will always be proud of the fact that I got the opportunity of a lifetime to serve my country as an officer in the Indian Navy. Some of the best and the worst memories of my life were with the Navy. I had been wearing my uniform every working day of my life for 17 years. It had become part of me, part of who I was, and it was time to leave all that. I had mixed feelings about it. I was excited about the future, but at the same time, worried that I would miss my life in the armed forces. I got more involved in the business and started giving all my time to it to keep myself busy.

Due to the downgrading of my medical category, my promotion to the rank of Commander had gotten delayed. Finally, my promotion letter came just weeks before my release date. In the Navy, we have a tradition called PLD, which means Pre-Lunch Drinks. This happens on a weekday, and it is held mainly to celebrate special occasions like promotions or farewells where we thank those who are leaving service (among others).

For promotions, we have an interesting tradition called 'Stripe Wetting' where the senior-most officer in the PLD would wet both the new stripes on the uniform with a few drops of beer. This gentlemanly gesture is soon followed by other senior officers, and by the time it comes to the turn of coursemates, the few drops would turn into mugs, and sometimes, the whole bottle. Though the tradition is called wetting the 'stripes', the wetting starts right from the head all the way down to the toes inside the shoes. Anyone at the receiving end gets beer-bathed that day. Now there is another tradition that happens when someone leaves service—a nice speech and a small gift in the form of a memento. In my case and maybe one of the rare cases, both happened together at one PLD. Thankfully my 'stripe wetting' by my coursemates happened after my farewell speech. Once PLD was over, everyone went back to their office, and I went back home 'retired'.

Luckily, I did not have much time to brood over the fact that I was now 'jobless' as two things kept me occupied. My daughter and my business. Just as in the first year as a cadet, where they did not give me time to think and miss my home and people, I did not get too much time to brood about my previous inning in the Navy. This period happened to be one of the best times of my life as I had something more precious than money-freedom. It was time-freedom. Once Giaa-Marie started going to pre-school, I used to go to pick her up and I would be the only dad among all the moms there. We would go to the malls during the afternoon on weekdays when it was not crowded, and all the rides would be empty. We went on road trips whenever we wanted. We visited tourist places during weekdays and avoided the weekend crowd. We worked hard and enjoyed hard as well. It was one of the best times of our lives.

Our teams were growing in different cities and countries. We had to split our energies to help our teams and decided that each of us would focus on certain markets as it was impossible for both of us to take care of all the markets. We then took a very difficult call to live separately for a couple of years as Pallavi was building Mumbai, Bangalore, and Dubai, and I was looking after the entire north of India. There was a need to be 'on the field' daily, especially in Mumbai and Delhi. Therefore, we decided that Pallavi would shift to Mumbai with Giaa and I would stay back in Delhi. I would visit them once or twice every month.

A REAL-LIFE MOVIE THAT HAPPENED IN FRONT OF ME

I had teams in many cities in the north of India and our core team decided to open other markets. One of the markets that kept coming up was Hyderabad. I put the plan in motion and that is when I remembered that Raju was now based in Hyderabad. I had lost touch with him after I got transferred to Pune Military hospital where I spent my last six months of hospitalisation. I knew that he had gone through a very rough patch where all his endeavours failed and people around him, even some of his near and dear ones, branded him as a 'failure'. There was a sense of helplessness in me when I used to think about him. Now, here was a chance where I could truly transform his life. Being financially free was not just a concept anymore for me. I had already done it and why wouldn't I do it for him?

I called him and the only thing I told him was that I was coming to Hyderabad, and I wanted him to trust me. I assured him that I will help him get out of all his financial troubles and even make him a millionaire. He told me in his ever-refined tone that we hadn't met in a long time and we would surely meet and discuss. He also told me that he would arrange for my stay and also pick me up from the airport. I agreed.

Once I landed at Hyderabad, I called the driver whose contact he had given, and he told me that he will reach in five minutes and that the vehicle was a red Pajero. I was quite impressed. I had come to know some years back that he was working as an employee in a company. Must be a great company to give their Pajero to pick up an employee's friend.

Once I got into the car, I called him and he told me that I could keep the vehicle if I wanted. I was a little surprised at this offer because, normally, company vehicles have their schedules, and I didn't know what he had to do to make that happen. Anyway, my meetings were scheduled for the entire day at one location. So, I did not need a car. He said he would come to my location in the evening.

I had multiple meetings and presentations for the day and even did one training. My meetings kept me busy till late evening. As I was winding up my day deep in a discussion with someone near the entrance of the hotel, I saw an Audi A4 model car come to the porch. Thanks to the movie *Transporter 2 & 3*, Audi had become my dream car and I had multiple pictures of it plastered on my dream-board back home. My jaw kind of dropped when I saw Raju getting out of it. There were people around talking to me, but I think I went blank. I ended the meetings and conversations as quickly as possible and got in his car. He had sent the driver home. It was just the two of us. I asked him in amazement, 'Raju, what is happening? How come you are driving my dream car?'

He smiled and told me, 'Let us get you settled and then we will talk.'

He drove into one of the finest 5-star hotels where he had booked a room for me. I dumped my luggage there and ventured out. My mind was on overdrive. I asked him eagerly, 'Raju, how come you are driving an Audi A4?'

He smiled and asked, 'Beems, is Audi your favourite car?' When I nodded my head vigorously, he said, 'Then let me give you a treat!'

He drove to a building, parked his A4 and got into another car. It was an Audi A7. I had had enough. I was brimming with excitement and happiness to see this 'movie' (as I always refer to it) unfold in front of me.

Finally, we got to his favourite restaurant where the main chef promptly came to him and took his order (which was not on the menu). We settled down and shared his story about how everyone had written him off, how he came to Hyderabad with a few hundred rupees in his pocket and how he built his multi-crore infrastructure business. He stayed with me at the hotel that night and we talked late into the night. I swell with pride every time I think about this incident because I had seen this kind of transformation only in Bollywood movies. I left Hyderabad totally inspired by Raju to make it big in my life.

Building any business takes a lot of effort, sweat, and tears. Pallavi and I gave it our everything. Since we were putting in so much, we were on the lookout for people who could help us invest our money further to get good returns. One of the beautiful things about this business is that there is no end to the kind of people you meet, and your circle of friends keeps growing. In normal life, we mostly meet people from similar walks of life because that is where we live and interact with people. However, here, there was no dearth to the variety of people I was meeting, and our circle kept growing.

During this time, Pallavi met a young and dynamic fund manager, Dhanunjay, who was working with a reputed investment firm in Mumbai. We were introduced to him through a very close friend, Maloni, whom we had met through the business. She also had invested money with him, and he was giving her good returns. I met him once briefly during one of my visits to Mumbai. Our friend was a qualified CA and understood finances and he came across as a soft-spoken individual who understood finances and investments. We were over the top of the world with joy and shared our dream of retiring financially by the time I turned 40, which was just a couple of years away. He assured us that it was very much possible, but we had to be aggressive about our investments. We were totally okay with the plan. It was better to suffer for a short period so that we could achieve our life goals. As Jim Rohn says, *'Do the things that you HAVE to do in the shortest period of time so that you can do the things you WANT to do for the longest period of time.'*

The next few years were all about frugal living. We started giving 80 to 90% of our earnings towards investments. He left the investment firm and started his own firm as he felt that he could serve his clients better by investing in foreign markets. He asked us if we would be willing to remove our funds from the investment firm where he was working and reinvest them in his company. He had been giving us good returns for the money that we had invested and there was no reason for us to doubt him or his intentions. We immediately withdrew all the funds and invested with him aggressively. He was very clear that he would divide the portfolio into low risk (50%), medium risk (30%) and on our insistence, he was willing to put 20% in high risk. We were insistent because we knew we had squandered a lot of money and we wanted to make up for it. Better to take a calculated risk than squander it.

In our network marketing business, we were part of a larger team and there were other leaders building their teams in different nodes. There was one person, Sajin, who started building his team very aggressively. He had prior experience in the industry but his ways were unseen and unheard of. They were not part of our team but part of the bigger team of which we were all a part. He became a hero to us. He was also a happy-go-lucky person, very friendly and always willing to help. He overtook all of us very soon in terms of team strength as well as earnings. We were more than willing to learn everything we could from him.

The challenge with network marketing is twofold. First is the fact that even though the parent company has clear guidelines about how to build the business, there is no control at the ground level as to how people do the business. The second big challenge was that during that time, there were no clear government directives or a regulatory body which this industry came under. So, all companies were in the grey area as far as the government was concerned. These two combined soon became like a volcano that was about to burst.

Now as Sajin's team started growing, a lot of people from some of the biggest and largest corporates joined his team. According to me, at some point, the team became over-ambitious, over-aggressive, and snobbish. His wife also started building the business along with him. However, she had different ideologies about how people were asked and approached regarding the business. Sajin operated from his heart. I believe he still does, even though he has reached stratospheric levels. I do have very good memories of interactions with him, and I respect him to date. When it came to his wife, Babita, I felt that she was all head about building the business and I could never identify with that. Her team went on overdrive and adopted practices that I still consider as unethical.

However, since she was getting results, it was my responsibility to check with my core team about how we were building the business. I discussed with my core team if we should adopt their strategies and I got a 100% vehement 'no' from everyone. When you become aggressive and start building teams fast, all the good things happen fast, and the challenges also happen fast. That is part of growth.

However, when you start living on the edge in terms of business ethics, it creates a lot of unwanted backlashes. People felt cheated and betrayed, even I would have felt the same if I were brought in a similar manner. Their business was growing at a breakneck speed, and they had no intention of slowing down. It reached a tipping point when people started to make official complaints, and law enforcement came down very heavily on the operations of the company.

We were kind of expecting this. It was inevitable. I was still in Delhi when this happened. The epicentre was in Mumbai, but the tremors were nationwide. Almost everything came to a standstill.

I had decided to shift to Mumbai by then. I had set up systems in Delhi and I had many leaders, some of whom were doing the business full-time. Also, Pallavi and I had had enough of living separately and wanted to live together. After all, we had been slogging for years now, and it was time to reap the benefits. I just didn't know that a bigger volcano was ready to burst, and we just were not prepared for it.

One of the first red flags was when Raju advised us not to put all our savings into just one type of investment. He asked some pertinent questions for which I did not have any answers. He then suggested that I take out all the money once, even if it's at a loss, and then redistribute it into different vehicles. When I told Dhanunjay that we wanted to take out all the money, he was not happy at all. He gave me a lecture on how my investments were tied to long-term deposits abroad and how we could not just take it out suddenly. Even when I assured him that we are good even if there were losses, there was no proper response from him. From that time onwards, he was not easy to reach, and my calls went unanswered many times.

I began to have uneasy feelings but kept myself positive because I could not even imagine the repercussions if anything went wrong. I had just decided to shift to Mumbai and be together with Pallavi and Giaa. I moved in with them into the flat in Goregaon West. I started on my coaching certification journey based on the insistence of a lot of my friends who said that since I was very good at mentoring and coaching others, I should get my certification and make it official. To be honest, I was more excited about the fact that after a couple of years, we were together.

One day, Maloni, who introduced us to Dhanunjay, called us to her place. All she told us was there was something very important to be discussed. It wasn't a casual call, and we could make it out from her voice. I remember feeling uneasy and uncomfortable but convinced myself that the gut feeling that I had been having for some time was not true. He had given us money from the interest of our investments to make a family trip to Hong Kong less than a year ago.

We reached her house and found a group of people sitting there, all looking very concerned. Some were familiar faces, and some were not, but the concern on everyone's face was real. Maloni started with the preface that she had been having a lot of issues with him and that she has not been able to trace any of the money that she had invested with him. She also had been asking him for money and he hadn't been responding. She did some investigation and prima facie, it appeared as though he had never even invested our money in any of the markets. It seems he was taking money from one person and giving part of it to someone else assuring them that it was the interest from their own investments.

I couldn't believe what I was hearing. I had the details of investments as well as the proof of investments into various companies as well as stocks. There was just one problem with all of them. They were all given by *him*, and I did not have the knowledge of how to authenticate the paper proofs that he had given us.

I could not stand. I felt weak in my legs, and I thought I might just fall. I just managed to sit down, and everything went blank for a minute. I could only hear Pallavi sobbing. We realised that we had messed up big, especially just a few months ago when we insisted that Pallavi's parents put their retirement money with Dhanunjay instead of keeping them in FDs which were giving hardly any returns. He came with us to Pune, sat in front of Papa and Mama, looked them in the eye and convinced them against their wishes to take out their retirement funds and invest with his company as it was the same as investing in FDs, but with better returns. He assured them that he would never risk their money.

Everyone was talking at the same time about lawsuits against him and how we should not spare him. The anger and frustration were palpable. Everyone had worked very hard for many years to make the money that they had given to this person in good faith. There was a lot of discussion about the future, and we all decided on one course of action—to try and get the money back from him. We fixed a date for that, and went home.

I could not say anything to comfort Pallavi. I was lost in thought. I *felt* lost and like a complete failure in life. We had worked so hard to make the money. I felt if I had put in even half the effort to learn and understand where I was investing our money, we would not be in such a state. It was all we had. If we could not get the money back, I would have to start from scratch. At 41 years of age, it didn't look good at all.

I don't think I have ever been so scared in my life. Not during my relegation, not during my accident and my stint in the ICU, not during the heartbreak. Back then, I was alone, and I was young. I was confident that I would be able to do something or the other. I knew that I could take care of myself somehow.

That was not the case right now. I was not alone anymore. I had a family. A wife and a child. It is easy to say that we were in this together, but I had certain expectations from myself. To be able to be the leader, provider, and protector of my family. Not to prove anything to anyone, but that is how I saw my role. I had failed in all three. I had not done my due diligence before giving all our money to him. I did not consult with anyone else who was an expert in this field, even though I had had access to many such people through my contacts. I had taken my life, my future, and our hard-earned money for granted.

However much I tried, I was not able to console myself or look at it logically. My entire life and our future looked bleak to me. I was thinking about retirement and was planning bigger things based on what we had earned and invested. There was no plan B. What started as our plan B became our plan A and the rest of the plans were dependent on this. I drew a blank. I had left service, the company that helped us create our wealth was going through their worst challenge in the country. Our teams had disintegrated or had taken a step back because of the challenge. We both were doing business full-time. We had left every other income-generating source we had, to pursue this with dedication.

And now this.

We also did not know how to break this news to Pallavi's parents who had given all they had based on our insistence that they deserved better returns. It is true that the road to hell is paved with good intentions. However, the intentions must be backed by solid actions, and in my case, the action required was financial education which was something I had never pursued. My depths of despair by then turned into anger. Anger towards this person who did not think twice before looting us of our life savings. Anger towards Maloni who knew things were not right but did not warn us even though she could have. It would have prevented us at least from putting our parent's money into this black hole. Anger at myself for being stupid and naïve, for not being responsible, for not doing my due diligence, for not being the protector of my family from people and events like these.

Pallavi's parents were shocked beyond words to know all that had happened. But just as parents are, they were more worried about *our* money than their own. This only made me even more furious. I was furious at God. This just was not fair. I had gone through enough deceit and let-downs. I had gone through a lot of physical, mental, and emotional pain. I had endured multiple operations, had to switch my career, left the Navy, and stayed away from my family to work towards our dream. After all this, he could not do something like this that affected not just me, but my entire family, bringing us to our knees. We were helping people change their lives. We had never been unethical in our business activities. I had never cheated anyone by telling them that they could make a profit without doing any work, and in our team, we ensured that no one joined the business before knowing what they were getting into.

It just did not make any sense. Why do bad things happen to good people? It's a million-dollar question, and in my case, it was a series of bad things.

Then on, my days became miserable as I found myself constantly thinking about the incidents and rethinking the different paths that I could have and should have taken. There was no peace, happiness, or excitement in the house anymore. We were shattered to the core.

One night, like many of the previous nights, I could not sleep, and I was on my usual trip of beating myself up and questioning everything I had done until then. I heard myself shouting, 'STOP!' It was weird. There was a part of me that was stronger than the 'why me?' part and I guess that part got tired of my constant whining. That part said, 'Bimal, it's just money. You have been through worse in life.' I couldn't understand what it meant. It was not just money. It was our entire life's savings. Yet somehow, I felt a certain peace in my mind, and I was able to sleep that night. I was determined to get out of my state of mind the next day.

There is a beautiful saying that goes, *'Courage is contagious. When a brave man takes a stand, the spines of others are stiffened.'* It is true with human faculties as well. When we decide to change our mindset, everything else starts shifting. The next morning, I decided to take charge of myself and my mindset.

The quality of our lives is defined by the quality of our decisions. I had a first-hand experience of this the next morning. Nothing had changed in my situation, but I woke up a positive and confident person. Someone with a totally different vibration. I realised that my state was not helping me or our family in any way. Someone had to be strong about the whole situation and the only person I could control and expect that of was me.

The toughest and most crucial step for me was to take 100% responsibility for what had happened. I realised that as long as I was blaming someone else, cribbing about how other people were or even justifying my mental and emotional state, I was preventing myself from moving forward in life. Life was going on. The sun rose and set every single day. People went on with their lives every single day. I could not be stuck in the past, no matter what happened. It wasn't easy at all, but it was the only way forward.

Once I was willing to accept 100% responsibility, the natural step forward for me was to ask, *'What Next?'* However, I realised that to reach this question, I had to take stock of all the events that had led to this incident so that it would never repeat in my life. For that, I had to retrace my steps to the beginning of my dealing with Dhanunjay.

One of the most glaring facts was that I was never interested in financial knowledge. I was good with numbers but not with complex financial transactions and I did not understand or care to understand the world of stock market investing or trading. I shrouded my lack of understanding or even interest in understanding by trust. I trusted Maloni, Maloni trusted Dhanunjay. So, I trusted Dhanunjay! I know it's laughable, but I was seeing the bare facts about this situation for the first time.

When you have a lot of money, it is cool to say that you have a 'fund manager' who invests the money wisely and gets you good returns. I didn't realise that even the people who say things like this would be watching their fund manager's actions very closely. I had taken everything for granted. I realised that I had left my goalpost unattended and if not him, someone else would have taken the shot at me. The hard fact was that I did not respect and take full responsibility for our hard-earned money. Why would it stay with someone who doesn't treat it well? It was a painful realisation for me. Ideally, this should have happened at least one year before. We could have saved so much more.

Now I could come to my life-changing question, *'What Next?'* I realised that to take the next step forward, I had to have clarity about exactly where I was standing. These were treacherous terrains and I had to be surefooted to avoid another fall, going forward.

I took stock of the current situation. There wasn't much to cling to or fall back on. Pallavi had left her profession at her peak to focus on the business full-time and build our teams. Since I had retired from the Navy pre-maturely, I was not eligible for any pension. We had some assets that we had made in the form of land and had some savings left. That was all. We had to start our life from scratch, along with a rented home in Mumbai and a child in school.

I looked at how I could possibly move forward in life. All I had were my skillsets. I had been mentoring and coaching people for many years. It was part of the business and teambuilding, where I had to wear multiple hats all through. I was mostly building their mindsets, handling their fears and self-doubt. Inadvertently, at times, I had to become a marriage counsellor and parenting coach and I have been helping a lot of people for many years. My team naturally looked up to me as their leader and counselled me for various aspects of their business as well as personal life. Many of my friends had been telling me that I should apply for a formal coaching certification so that I could help a larger number of people.

One thing that we learned in our journey of personal development was that one should never stop investing in themselves. We can only earn to the extent that we grow ourselves. I decided to invest in my coaching certification. We identified one of the best coaching methodologies on the planet through one of our business partners, Soum, who had spent more than 30 years in some of the top corporates at the CXO level. He was impressed with my people and mentoring skills. Once he also put the stamp that my life was meant to be spent helping others, I decided to take up coaching professionally. I reached out to Coaching and Leadership International (CLI) based in Canada, and even though we did not have the means, they were willing to take me on with a payment plan. This turned out to be one of the best decisions of my life because the skills I learned from there have helped me transform thousands of lives, some through one-on-one coaching and others through my training. I also completed my NLP certification during this time.

Even though our situation had not changed, and we had not started earning in any big way, our lives began to change. We were looking ahead, seeing possibilities, and working on moving forward, and that made all the difference.

What was my learning from this whole fiasco? There were many. The first and most important one was about money. Financial education is something that is not taught in schools or colleges. Something that I have been teaching my child from a very young age. *The purpose of earning money is not to spend it but to invest in assets that will continue to bring in money.* I believe that this must be taught and drilled into every child while they are growing up so that when they start earning, they have the right mindset towards money. They should enjoy the money, yes, but they should also learn to invest a part of it.

❖ ❖ ❖

Another big learning was to do my due diligence, especially where money was concerned. If I really respect the money I have, I should learn to invest it. Having money is like having a child. Just because I didn't have any prior experience, I would not hand my child over to someone else to raise her. Even if I make a mistake, it would be my decision and my mistake.

The fact was that I had not taken 100% responsibility for my finances. At one end was learning about investments, but at the other extreme was my willingness to take important decisions with strangers based on 'trust'. It is good to trust people but there must be some logic behind the trust. My lack of understanding of financial markets and my unwillingness to even try and understand it made me the perfect target for people who could use big words and excellent projections to seduce me into 'trusting' them. Well, in God, you trust. Rest all, you test before you trust. One of my mentors always said *the trust that is not tested is not real trust.*

Another big learning was never to put all my eggs in one basket. Even though we were doing well in the business, it had become our only source of income. Also, we were investing all the money into one place only. Two cardinal mistakes. We should have leveraged other sources of income as well, even if it was just to keep the craft alive, like coaching or training. In our case, we had left everything else based on 'sound advice' from some of the mentors in the business. Therefore, when we faced a challenge, starting fresh was like pushing a car up a hill. It was tough.

One thing that didn't let me down was all the training and coaching that I had invested in during the business. I had grown tremendously as an individual, as a leader, team player, trainer, and coach. I was exposed to the world of personal development, and it completely changed my mindset about who I could be and what was possible for me. If it was not for this, I don't think I would have even been able to get out of a crisis of this magnitude.

There is always a 'next' for every one of us. No matter what the circumstances may be. It may look like the darkest day and the end of the road, but if we are willing to ask ourselves the very important question, 'What Next?', a new world of opportunities opens out for us. The very fact that we are ready to ask this question is a clear indication to the universe as well as to ourselves that we are ready to move forward in life. That we are ready to let go of the past and look to the future.

Unfortunately, a lot of people are not willing to ask this question because they are unable to think outside their situation and figure out how to get out of it. The only reason why they cannot get out of the situation is that they choose not to. The moment they ask this question, the responsibility of life falls squarely back on their shoulders and that is scary for most, if not all. They prefer to live inside the four walls of denial, blame, justification, and self-pity, and watch their entire life pass them by, and for some, by the time they realize their mistakes, it may well be too late to take corrective actions.

Asking 'What Next?' puts the power back in your hands. It fills you with confidence and positive expectation as it is a clear indication to your subconscious as well as to the universe that, the incident is over, and you are done with it.

A keynote, though. 'What Next' is not something to be asked only during setbacks. It is equally important to ask this once you have achieved a goal. Many people reach a goal and then deteriorate in life because they don't ask this question. This question propels them to set new goals that put them on the path to greater heights and achievements. People who have achieved great feats in life have constantly asked this question to keep growing and moving forward.

An interesting aspect of this question is that the more you use it, the better you get at it. You will get out of your challenges much quicker; you will not feel like you are 'finished' due to tough incidents as you will subconsciously know that it is not the end of the road for you. Yes, you will go through a period of brooding and that is perfectly human, but the duration will lessen, and your turnaround time will also keep getting better. 'What next?' is your bounce-back muscle. The more you exercise it, the better you get at it and the stronger you become.

CHAPTER 12

OPPORTUNITIES FIND YOU!

If you truly believe, dreams do come true.

This was my Facebook update when I proudly shared the post about launching my tech company. It truly was a dream coming true for me. Not only was I a co-founder of a tech startup, but it was with two of my closest friends. One was Ramki, a tech genius, and the other was Raju, an astute entrepreneur.

This was immediately after the incident where I lost all my life savings. Once I decided to take full responsibility and move forward in life, I received an unexpected call from a long-time friend, Ramakrishna (Ramki, who was the mainstay in the Naval Pay Office project). He had left the Navy almost the same time as I did and was working in an MNC in Delhi. While we were together at the Naval headquarters, we used to hang out on the rooftop during our breaks talking about this and that and something in between, and he would talk about all the latest things in the tech world. In 2007, we discussed cloud computing. Well, it was more like him educating me. He told me that it would change the world.

Even though I had done my certification as an Oracle DBA and was still posted in an IT role, I had lost interest in working in the IT domain. What excited me most was personal development, helping people achieve their dreams and aspirations through the business. I realised that I thrived when I was teaching, training, and coaching people. I could help them see the potential that they could not see in themselves. I could take them to a higher level of day-to-day functioning. Even though I was an introvert by nature, I truly was a people person.

This was not the first time that Ramki had called with a business idea. When he had pitched the last one, we had met a friend of ours based in Mumbai. However, it did not take off since all of us felt that the execution was going to be difficult. When Ramki shared his new idea with me, I could immediately see the possibilities and how it could empower small businesses to get online with just a smartphone. It was quite a revolutionary idea and something that had great potential.

When I took stock of my life situation, I could see that while I had just lost my entire life savings, once I changed my outlook towards life and started asking the question 'What Next?', I could see new doors opening for me. It's like the saying that if you drive a car looking only at the rear-view mirror, you will miss out on everything that is in front of you. The moment I stopped my self-pity and brooding, my coaching certification, NLP[43] and now a new business idea, all of them, opened up for me. Try it out. It works every time.

Once I went through the business plan, I was on board with the idea. When it comes to business, I follow one principle. Never

---

[43]Neuro-linguistic programming (NLP) is a pseudoscientific approach to communication, personal development and psychotherapy that can help you achieve specific goals in life.

bet on an idea. Always bet on the people behind the idea because it's people who decide the outcome of the idea. I knew Ramki well enough to know that he had the attitude, skills, and knowledge to deliver on his idea. We still needed someone who could fund the startup since I was wiped out and he was an employee. The natural choice was Raju. Even though technology was not his core focus, I felt that it was a win-win situation as both could benefit from each other. I spoke with Raju, and he also wanted to know more about Ramki than the idea. I knew that once Raju saw the business plan, we would know immediately if he was interested or not. He was not one of those people who would gather information, mull over it for a day or two and then take a decision. His decisions have always been immediate and spot-on. We had a formal meeting in Delhi to discuss the business plan and within 15 minutes of the presentation, Raju was on board as well.

Ramki and I travelled to Hyderabad frequently for further discussions. Hyderabad was the default choice for setting up operations as both Raju and Ramki were from Hyderabad (though Ramki was settled in Delhi, his hometown was Hyderabad), and that left me with no choice other than to move to a city that was never in my consideration to settle down. Today, after many years, I think this was another one of my best decisions. Today I am happily settled here, which has become one of the most progressive and growth-oriented cities in India.

This, for me, was starting life from scratch. Like losing a year in the Navy that changed my career path, my accident that took my life on a different path, the fiasco with my 'fiancée', which turned out to be a blessing later, losing my life savings and many other incidents that I have not even covered in this book, this was another reset and restart for me. I know of people who get all flustered because their office cubicle was changed to a new one. I really do not know of too many people who have had to start life from scratch so many times.

My life experiences had taught me by now that I need to embrace opportunities that came my way, and I was confident this time and ready for the next adventure and whatever it had in store for me. I also knew that this particular one was innovative and path-breaking. It was exciting to be part of something new. I jumped headfirst into my role as the Head of Marketing and Sales.

This was not a part-time job. No startup can be a part-time job, especially when you decide to hire full-time employees. We initially worked in a small and dingy conference room in Raju's Infra company. This also meant that I had to shift my family to Hyderabad. As I was busy with our new startup, Pallavi had been taking care of our daughter as a full-time mom and homemaker. It was not a tough decision for them to move to Hyderabad. We found a nice house and we moved in there. I was working late hours during the week, and we spent most of our time together during weekends. We went out to the malls, movies, and regular stuff that a family does, and life was good.

When I'm entrusted with a task, I do not know how to give less than my 100% to it. This was the first time I was in a corporate set-up, and I had to come up with a sales and marketing plan for a product that was still only on paper. I was very excited about what the future held for us and the product that we were developing. Most of my time went into research. I still have a folder full of ideas and plans that I had conceived, inspired by innovative companies and their best practices, which were then tailored to suit our needs. No one has seen the folder and the ideas other than me to date because I could never implement them. A lot of it had to do with customer engagement and retention and we never reached that stage with our company.

Fast forward to August 2017. I was driving back home that evening and I had tears flowing down my cheeks, blurring my vision. I could not get myself to play the stereo which used to dish out Arijit Singh songs during my drives to and from my office. It was the end of my dream, in fact, our collective dream, that had started two years back. I was returning from my last day in the office as we shut our office, winding up the startup. I had watched as the watchman switched off the lights of an empty office and closed the door for the last time. It was like watching a young athlete breathing his last.

The office had bustled with energy, laughter, ideas, and discussions all this time. From just the three of us at the start, we had grown to a strength of more than 150 at our peak. We had the best advertising agency in the country working for us. We had a full-fledged tech team, a design team, social media and marketing team, a tele-calling team, and a field sales team. We had opened our office in Bangalore as well. We had team bonding sessions, Sunday cricket matches, and team lunches once a month, and I had also regularly imparted my personal training to my sales team. It was full of energy and action.

How could such a dream die? That too just weeks before the official launch? Who is to be blamed? I still don't have an answer to it. Both Raju and Ramki are still close friends, Raju is more like a brother to me. Maybe it was my fault. Since I was close to both of them, I was not able to take a firm stand, even though I tried even that towards the end.

By then, it was too late. The fact is that Ramki and Raju were both brilliant. Ramki had a vision which was based on technology and Raju's vision was based on reaching those people who did not even have the technology (at least at the time). To cut a long story short, we could not agree on a common goal and path forward. It was better to put an end to it rather than wait for a few years, by which time the idea would have grown into a big business. It would have been difficult and ugly then. The good news is that our friendship is still intact, which is a big deal because Raju did spend a huge amount of money on this company since he was funding it single-handedly and it would have made anyone else quite angry and bitter. I truly believe that the app would have helped so many small businesspeople, even those working in remote areas to have a better life.

Once everything was done and over and we parted ways, I realised that I was staring at starting again from scratch, with a family to look after. Raju went overboard to help me out and kept me on his payroll, moving me into another company owned by him. Ramki went on to start his tech firm and is doing well for himself today.

Naturally, my next question was 'WHAT NEXT'. By this time, it had become the most natural step forward for me. I had to focus on my life ahead, instead of what didn't happen. I again took stock of my strengths, and I realised one important thing. My life after leaving the Navy had been all about personal development, mentoring and coaching. I was also into sales in a big way, but I had not enjoyed it much. I was more of the knowledge-giver/solution-provider kind.

Around that time, a seminar called *Millionaire Mind Intensive (MMI)* came to Hyderabad for the first time. I had heard about T Harv Eker and this program in 2005, when I discovered the amazing world of personal development. They did not have the program in India at that time, but I had set a strong intention to do it sometime.

I am also a believer in signs from above (as I call them). At times, you encounter things in life that you haven't really planned for. This could be good or bad. Once I go through any experience, and I think back and realise that it was not a planned one and it had just happened, then I know that it was meant/not meant for me. This has happened to me multiple times. The information about MMI came to Pallavi through a random WhatsApp message. She still doesn't remember who had sent it to her. When she shared it with me, I felt that it was one of those signs. A calling for an intention I had left in 2005. We decided to go for it.

MMI is a three-day program and if you have not done it yet, make sure you do it. It will have a huge impact on your life (not just financially). There I also realised all the mistakes that we had done when we had a lot of money. It was not easy for both of us to re-live the past and go through the emotions and feelings that we had been through at that time. However, the experience was quite liberating for us. At the end of three days, we were offered a package called Quantum Leap which was a bundle of courses which would take our education with T Harv Eker even further. We instinctively knew that this was the answer to our situation. They were offering a full progression into personal development as well as giving us an International Trainer Certification, which would help us take our life forward as trainers, our core strength. However, the price was way more than what we could afford at the time. We just had enough money to put in the initial deposit and we decided to swipe our cards with the belief that if this was meant for us, money would show up.

This is also the place we met Surendran Jayasekar, fondly referred to as Suren. He is the owner of Success Gyan, the largest seminar organizing company in India. He is one of the most amazing human beings I have come across in my life. He has grown to become a close friend and mentor over the years. His mission in life is to make India the training capital of the world and he is relentless in his pursuit of this goal. In spite of that, he is brutally honest. He would be the first one to tell those who gets overenthusiastic to sign up for the courses without a clear idea, that the course is not apt for them. He advices them to focus on something else that is their strength. People find it difficult to digest the fact that he says no to those who offer him money to do his courses but that is who he is. He told us clearly that if training was our goal, the courses were not only required for us, but since we were good at our craft, it was also a great opportunity as he was looking for high-quality trainers whom he also wanted to promote.

We knew money wasn't going to drop from the sky, for sure. But I guess we were meant to do it because people came forward to help us. My in-laws, who asked us to take whatever was required from them, Raju, whom we, as a family, can never thank enough for all the help and support he has given us all through our lives, and whatever savings we were left with, helped us do the courses.

The trainer certification course was Train the Trainer (TTT), and it was conducted by Blair Singer. I am yet to come across someone so magnetic, authentic, and transparent as him. Anyone who has been trained by Blair will vouch for this. Everyone falls in love with him. He becomes a mentor and father figure to everyone. He is rightly called 'The Magician' because he has been able to train and create world-class trainers and most of the famous international trainers were trained by him at some point in their journey.

During TTT, we were offered a course called Making the Stage (MTS) which was the highest level of training in the training industry. In this course, we would be personally coached (while we are on stage delivering our content) by some of the best trainers and coaches in the world. We again trusted the universe for the provision and registered for that as well. We ended up going for that course, thanks to Raju again and my in-laws. The night I reached I was down with diarrhoea. I could not afford to miss even a minute of the 5-day training for which we had paid a lot and had made a lot of sacrifices. Despite my condition, I was determined to give it my best possible shot. I got better as the days passed and each day, I gave my all. Pallavi and I hardly saw each other because we were in different groups and the timings were brutal. We started at 0900h each morning and ended around 0200 or 0300h the next morning. Sleep and food only got in the way.

At the end of five days, after our final presentations, Suren gave us the awesome news that both Pallavi and I were selected to be trainers for MMI. This was huge because, from the time MMI came to India in 2014, they were looking for Indian trainers who had the calibre to be on the T Harv Eker platform. We both had made it and it was indeed a big moment for both of us. One of us had to choose the path and Suren suggested that I do it since the travel would be extensive and training would be even more intensive and away from home.

Part of becoming an MMI trainer was to be Blair Singer Training Academy certified (BSTA). Blair's trainings covered every aspect of training, personal development, team building, facilitating, coaching and much more. The most comprehensive training curriculum in the world for any trainer. I was more than happy as being part of BSTA was already on my bucket list, and now, it had become mandatory.

While we were doing our initial courses which were part of the Quantum Leap package, we were clear that we didn't want to be just corporate trainers. We wanted to have something that we called our own. Our signature program. I knew it had to be on parenting even though it was not crystal clear to me then. As time passed and as I started working on it, I realised that I have been studying parenting for over 20 years, thanks to the incidents that I saw while I was in my hospital bed in Kolkata, way back in 1998.

❈ ❈ ❈

Allow me to take you back once again to 1998 to my hospital bed. My bed was in intensive care which was right next to the nurses' station. Patients used to come and go, and I was the sole long-term occupant among the four beds. Most of the people who used to occupy the bed next to mine were retired, elderly officers who were close to 70 years of age, while I was in my 20s.

The thing about old and retired *faujis* is that they like to talk a lot. They have so many interesting incidents in their lives to talk about, and they love an audience. They found me literally tied to my bed and they used to talk to me the whole day about various things. About their career, their family, and life in general.

Initially, I used to get irritated. I was already in so much discomfort and the last thing I wanted was to hear their life stories. I mean, I was just starting my life. *Why don't they spare me?* I thought. Soon, I realised that they were talking from 65 or 70 years of life experience and that is when I started listening to them.

My turning point happened because of two people who came one after the other on the bed right next to mine. First was a senior officer who retired as a Commodore. He was a highly decorated officer for his contributions to the Navy. A lean, tall officer.

Whenever he used to talk to me about his career, his face used to light up. He would tell me amazing things about all that he did in his career, but when it came to talking about his family, he was sad. He was a localite and his wife used to come and meet him in the evening. He had two sons who were working in an IT company there, and I did not see them even once during his two-week stay in the hospital.

One afternoon, he was quite emotional, and he told me, 'Bimal, I achieved a lot in my career and I'm proud of it. But if I had to do it all over again, I would do it differently. I would put my family first and make sure that I spend more time with my kids. If I had done that, today when I need them, they would have been here for me. Don't make this mistake in your life.'

I felt sad for him as I could see the sadness on his face. He got discharged after a couple of weeks.

After he got discharged, the next officer who came on the same bed had retired as a Lieutenant Commander which means he didn't achieve great heights in his career. He was pot-bellied, used to crack jokes all the time and made everyone laugh. Every single evening, there used to be a large crowd who came to meet him. His two daughters, sons-in-law, and grandkids. The kids used to literally climb on him. They left only when the duty nurse insisted that they leave as the visiting time was over. This happened every single day for the two weeks that he was there. It was delightful to see all of them talking at the same time and the kids vying for his attention all the time. He didn't know about the conversation I had with the officer before him.

One of those afternoons, he spoke with me. He said, 'Bimal, I did well in my career, I worked hard, and gave my everything but may not have reached a high rank. I was more of a family man all through, and today my daughters love me so much that they don't let me buy even my pyjamas[44]. At this stage of my life, what more can I ask for? There is nothing more important in life than having a close and happy family.'

This incident hit me like another truck because I had seen the other side just before him. I could not sleep that night despite my painkillers and sedative. I was in the prime of my youth and totally career-focused at that time. For me, then, the ultimate goal in life was achieving success in my career and earning a lot of wealth. However, I was witnessing real-life examples of two totally opposite approaches to life. We don't usually get to see this. While we are young, we don't have the time and patience to sit and learn about life from those who have been there and done that. And by the time we get to learn, more often than not, it's too late.

After this incident, lying on my hospital bed, I decided that my primary goal in life must be to have a loving and happy family. Everything else would be secondary to that. That is when I started studying how to develop loving relationships within a family and how to bring up kids in such a way that they remained connected to me for the rest of my life. I've read hundreds of books, researched extensively, read white papers, met psychologists, did my child and family counselling certification and more. However, I never had the intention of teaching this to anyone. I was purely doing it out of my desire for my family (which was non-existent at that time).

Therefore, I knew clearly that I wanted to teach parenting from all that I had learned. It was also reassuring to see how I was able to develop a strong bond with my daughter because I was implementing all that I learned. I was also seeing the other side in many cases around me.

---

[44]Pyjamas are night wear clothes. Also called as PJs, jammies, jam-jams, or night suits.

However, I did not want to teach basic or vague concepts about parenting. Parenting training are mostly piecemeal. Some are about 'happy parenting', some are about 'mindful parenting', some talk about communication, and some about setting boundaries and rules. I wanted to develop a scientific approach to parenting. I wanted to develop a framework on parenting that can be applied to all families and help them irrespective of the challenges they are facing. Something that addresses the parent-child relationship at a grassroots level instead of 'handling issues' or handling just one or two aspects of parenting. I tried different models, and I was not happy the way it was shaping up because I was not able to find a natural connection between the modules in the models.

One day I was studying *Maslow's Hierarchy of Needs* for human beings. It is a simple yet profound theory that applies to all human beings. It simply says that there is a hierarchy of needs for human beings and unless the most basic and fundamental needs are addressed, you cannot move comfortably to the next level.

For me, this was the missing link. I realised that there is a hierarchy of needs for our kids as well. Parents need to address the fundamental needs first before they try to implement other aspects of parenting. For example, everyone talks about how important communication is with kids. Now I believe that, for effective and fruitful communication to happen, it is important for the parent and child to have a deep connection based on trust and respect. If the child doesn't trust the parent to be honest and open, the communication tends to become a lecture (which kids hate). That is how I came up with my '*6Cs of Parenting Principles*'. It became a three-day live workshop where all the parents who attended were transformed by the third day. This was and is something very close to my heart. The first batch is always special, and interestingly, we have become like one big family. They still reach out to me for any guidance, and we meet often and celebrate occasions together.

I had to slow down my workshops as I was also being mentored and trained to become the first ever trainer from India for MMI. I travelled a lot as ATT (Assistant Trainer in Training) and assisted in a lot of MMIs, not just in India but in many other Asian countries as well. All this travel was at my own expense since I had not yet been confirmed as an AT. This was an amazing year where I met so many different people from all walks of life across several countries. International flights, visa, hotels to stay in, nothing was cheap. All this travel also meant that I was burning through all my savings and whatever little I had. Our logic was to do as many seminars as possible with different crowds so that the journey to become an AT gets shortened. Finally, after more than a year of travelling and assisting MMIs as ATT, I got a call to be the Assistant Trainer for MMIs in Singapore and Vietnam. It meant that they would take care of all my expenses, and I would also get paid for my services. All the efforts for the past few years, all the investments I had made in terms of efforts, time and money were finally coming to fruition. We were ecstatic as a family.

Two weeks before the MMI in Singapore, India went into lockdown due to Covid-19.

CHAPTER 13

THE PREDICAMENTS IN A PANDEMIC

Am I really such a bad person that God just wouldn't let me do anything that I set my mind to? My career in the Navy, my girlfriend, my life savings, my start-up and now, all that I worked so hard for was also going down the drain. It looked as if God was picking on me specifically, and I had no clue what I had done to deserve it. I was into live training. MMI crowds tend to run into anywhere between 800 to a couple of thousands. Pallavi's career revolved around live events. Covid brought both these to a grinding halt. Full stop to every single thing that we had been working towards and were looking forward to over the last two years.

I did not have anything online going on. My personal coaching had taken a backseat because it required me to invest a lot of time in it, and like with everything else, I take coaching seriously. Now that Covid had brought the entire world to a halt, coaching was one of the last things people wanted. No one knew what to expect or how things were going to be, and everyone was holding on to whatever savings they had just so they could get through this Covid period.

I am a strong person. I have been through many major challenges in my life, even beyond what has been covered in these pages. But to be honest, I was tired, frustrated, angry and upset when this latest disappointment happened. I knew I had to ask myself 'What Next?', but I didn't want to. I was in no state of mind because I was tired of going through challenges and digging my way out every single time. It was time for me to experience the 'good and easy life' that I had been working for, that had eluded me this far. To have loads of money, to have the time to spend with my family, to buy my favourite cars, to go on vacations with Pallavi and Giaa-Marie. It wasn't too much to ask, I thought. I had been working my backside off, I had been giving my everything to every setback, every challenge, every new beginning. It is said that there is a time to sow and then there is a time to reap. How long was I to keep sowing? Would I ever get a time to reap in this lifetime? It wasn't fair. It just was not. Period. I just wanted to crawl into my bed and sleep for a long, long time. And to be honest, I did that for almost a month.

The challenge with savings is that when you take from it, it keeps dwindling. I realised this in a month. Whether I liked it or not, I had to take some action. My time to grieve was over. Life did not stop; days did not stop dawning. Life was chugging along as if nothing had happened. It was up to me to do something about it.

It was time to ask, *'What Next?'*. I knew all the while that I would not only have clarity about the next steps, but that I would be able to move forward only after asking and answering this question.

The most important thing to remember is that you can ask this question only when you are mentally and emotionally ready to move forward. Without that, the question does not have the power and capability to get you out of your challenge. For me, it was at this point.

I had to look at my harsh reality and accept it. Trainings were not going to happen for a long time. I realised that the only way forward is to go online. One of the things I used to do was to go on an evening walk with Uma, my best friend. She had been telling me for a while to start online courses on parenting and I had been arguing with her because my live trainings had some powerful processes that totally changed the way parents looked at their children and their role as parents. It was powerful because it was a controlled environment, and I could create the right context to lead them towards the transformation they were seeking. I believed I would not be able to create the same environment online.

Well, that argument got settled, thanks to Covid. We decided to work together and put up the online course. I had the full content ready for the live workshop. We just needed to figure out what needed to be changed to make it equally effective online. This again required investments into camera, lights, and a host of other investments. And like every single time, Raju helped me out. He was truly my lifesaver during this time. Pallavi had been doing an amazing course for kids which was getting fantastic results and feedback. She also decided to take the course online.

In the next few months, I completely focused on building the course. I used to work from Uma's home as we were working on it together and we could make sure that we worked for long hours without even taking a break. The amazing Tam Brahm[45] (short for Tamil Brahmins) filter coffees that I got whenever I wanted was a total bonus and incentive to work in her house. The good thing

---
[45] Tamil Brahmins are an ethnoreligious community of Tamil-speaking Hindu Brahmins, predominantly living in Tamil Nadu

about working with someone likeminded is that we can bounce off ideas, we can argue and fight about a concept till one of us convinces the other. It worked like a charm because we both were bull- headed and stubborn when it came to bringing up children. She was already sold on the 6Cs of parenting principles because our arguments regarding each C had happened long ago, mostly during our walks.

At times, she would share a challenge about a child or a family that she'd read or heard about, and we would try to figure out which C was not in place and why it was not in place. She had been a journalist and writer all her life and had worked with the best in the business which helped her connect with some amazing people. Through her, we were able to add tremendous value to our course by having real life examples of fathers, mothers, grandparents, child specialists, and other parenting experts. We both are people who appreciate when we see or come across something of real value and had been looking at various parenting workshops and courses when we realised that what we had created was excellent. It was foundational and comprehensive, and we could peg all the other courses that we came across as subsets of what we had created.

It was a lot of hard work getting the course online. The script had to be changed, we had to bring in more value since processes had to be taken out. We had to make the presentations which thankfully, Uma said she would. I do have this niggling thought that it was also because she knew I wouldn't do a good job with it. We reached out to our contact circles and brought in national and international experts in every single area that was required for parenting. From cybersecurity, social media, bullying, health, fitness, nutrition, yoga, sex education, addictions and suicides, LGBTQIA, spiritualism, money management, and many more, every single area was covered through interviews with the experts.

Our goal was to ensure that everything that a parent needed to know for bringing up children was covered, and we did it, and dare I say, we did it beautifully.

We launched our course and had parents signing up for it. Those who did the course diligently experienced great transformations in their families, especially in the relationship with their children. Part of the course bundle was a weekly call to know what was happening and how things were going for them. If they came across some specific challenges, we would address it during these calls. I chose parenting because it was my passion and I'd been studying it, and living it for almost two decades. It was never about making a fortune with it. At least, the thought had never crossed my mind. I had started teaching parenting while I was trying to be a trainer for MMI which was to be my main career.

A few months down the line, I realised one thing. Parenting was one of the hottest topics, especially after the pandemic. Every parent understood the need for it, and the importance of it, but only a few were willing to pay to learn parenting. I realised that it had a lot to do with mindsets. I think someone paid for a parenting course, it somehow connotated to them that they were bad parents. It is a similar thing to mental health. Everyone talks about it, but no one openly goes to a mental health professional, which is very sad. On top of that, conducting webinars required money for ads and other forms of marketing. It was like walking on a rope. At one point, I decided to give my webinars a break as I could not afford to burn through any more of our last bit of savings.

This was also the time when one of my good friends, Dinesh, who was also my coachee[46], came home to gift me the book that he

---

[46]**One who is coached** (receives coaching)

had written. He asked me if he could speak with me openly and I told him, 'Of course.'

He gave me quite a mouthful but in a decent and respectful way. He told me that I was wasting my potential trying to reform parents. He said I had done a great thing getting the course done but now I had to focus on my core strength, which was leadership coaching and mindset building, because that was what I had done all my life. He also insisted that I write a book on it. I could literally see Uma rolling her eyes because she had been telling me to write a book for over a year by then. Anyway, all this helped, and I decided to start writing this book. For me, starting something sometimes takes time. Once I start, I can move fast.

I also decided to focus on my coaching. My certification had been pending for a while as I had to submit many documents to receive it and I had postponed it for quite a while. I got down to it and submitted all my documents and got my Certified Power Coach certification. I am especially proud of this because I have never come across a coaching methodology as powerful as this. I have seen miracles happening during my coaching sessions—people identifying the root cause of their challenges as some events happened to them when they were in college, in their teen years and even as young as five years old. The results I have been seeing with my clients were amazing. It was as if I am taken over by a higher power during my sessions, prompting me to ask the right questions leading them to get their breakthroughs. I decided to take it up and focus on it with the help of Uma. I officially launched myself as a Mindset Mentor and Executive Coach through my website bimalraj.com. Today apart from working with a renowned corporate, I also train teams, do one-on-one executive coaching and counsel parents and teenagers.

Well, that is my story. At least thus far. Are you disappointed reading this? Did you expect to read a story about how I overcame my odds and became a millionaire? Well, I was one! Remember? I see bookstores filled with books of how people became millionaires, books that teach you how to become one yourself. I see ads after ads on Facebook about how you can become a millionaire and have your dream life if you woke up at 5:00 am, if you just follow the steps that they teach you, if you attend their course, et cetera.

I have nothing against any of them or what they teach. I am no one to comment on what anyone has to offer. It may work, or it may not, but I firmly believe, and know, that it is all up to *you* and how you make it work for you. Also, remember that no one teaches you how to manage your millions once you get there. I have been there, done that. I have enjoyed time-freedom as well as money-freedom. I've travelled to different countries with my family for holidays, have driven from Delhi to Trivandrum in Kerala, that too taking 45 days, not because I had a slow car, but because I had both time as well as money freedom. It is a great feeling to be in that space. The most important education that you need to have is to learn how to bounce back if you lose all of it because challenges are part of life, part of growth, and part of who you become in your journey towards earning millions.

Have I given up wanting to be back there? Definitely not. I remember Raju telling me once that he wanted to see me do something big. Those words are etched in my heart, and I am always on the lookout to fulfil his belief in me and my abilities. Should you give up on your dreams and aspirations? Of course not. This book was never about making you a millionaire or how to achieve your dream life. This book is for those who may have gone through challenges, those who might go through them in the future. Irrespective of who you are and what you do, one thing is for certain. You will go through some challenges. This can be physical, mental, emotional, financial, and what have you. Some people like me could go through a buffet of all of them.

You will recall from the first chapter that I had a lovely childhood. Loving parents and elder sisters who were mothers to me. A protected life where I was always with my parents. Once, my uncle suggested to my parents that I should be put in a hostel, and I remember having nightmares and crying and pleading with my mom not to send me away from them. Why am I telling you this? Because I was a pampered and protected child, with people around me always, to make sure that I didn't face major challenges. If I could transform from that state to the current one, where I coach people on how to get through challenges and be successful in life, I need you — well, I want you — to know that anyone can go through incredible transformations. I truly believe that. You may be seeing things only one way when there are at least ten other ways to look at it. So, if you went through a challenge and are unable to shake the effects or the ill feelings off, or are not able to come out of the pit that you are in, I want you to trust yourself and ask yourself the golden question, *'What Next?'*

Yes, it may not be as simple as it sounds. Which is why I am giving you the tools to break it down so you can get clarity on how to ask this question and how to move forward in life.

Are you ready to ask yourself, ***'What Next?'***

CHAPTER 14

THE WHAT NEXT MINDSET

It is said that the biggest war ever fought and one you will ever fight is the one between your two ears. It is the greatest battle, the battle with the self. I was trained for four years to be ready for war by the best in the business—the Indian Armed Forces. But none of that training prepared me for the war that I had to wage with myself. Yes, there is always a certain level of mental toughness that military training imparts. Many people think that military training is all about physical fitness. I have realised that the body is the first to give up. When I ran cross-country every Sunday, my physical fitness took me just about halfway, for about eight kilometres. The rest of it was all in the mind. I constantly had to figure out a way to keep moving forward because I didn't have a choice but to finish on time.

There is nothing more important in life than having the right mindset. It's the right mindset that makes a person successful in life. If you don't have the right mindset, you may attend a training, might implement the learning but still be unsuccessful or less successful than someone else who attended the same training with you but had a stronger mindset. Does that make you a loser? Definitely not. You just need to identify and understand who you are and where your heart lies. Don't ever be pressurised by other people's expectations.

Life will always throw different challenges and curve balls at you. Some manageable and some crippling. At that point, you need to realise that you are being challenged and stretched. You need to take a decision that you will not break under the weight of it. You always have the choice of reclaiming your life and your happiness or letting yourself crumble under self-pity, uncertainty, fear, procrastination, frustration and many more negative emotions and thoughts that will spiral you all the way down into a pit of deep despair and depression.

Irrespective of the kind of state you are in, you need to know deep down that you have the power and the ability to take small steps towards recovery and reclaim a life of joy and purpose. You can make all the negativity that you may be feeling right now shrink, until they are no longer there. I was watching the movie *The Amazing Spiderman 2* and one line from the famous speech by Gwen sums it up. She says, '*We have to be greater than what we suffer.*'

Depending on what you have gone through, you may feel totally bewildered by too many questions and uncertainties. For me, the biggest was being wiped out financially when I was around 40. I didn't know where to start, how to start, what to do, how to plan the future, what immediate steps to take. There were too many things overwhelming me. It took me a while to get rid of the clouds before I was able to think clearly.

This 'What Next' method can help you and guide you in getting out of your situation, whatever it may be. The aim is not to give you all the solutions to your problems, but for you to get to a stage where you can think clearly and logically so you can find your own solution. Once you reach that stage, you will be fine because you have all the solutions within yourself. It is your life, your experiences, your strengths, and your weaknesses. You are the best judge of the best steps to take to move forward. I'm not saying this to inspire you. This is a fact. I have been coaching for years and I have seen people coming up with solutions to seemingly impossible situations when their thought processes became clear. Trust me when I say this. You have the solutions to move forward, and you also have the ability to get out of this situation. It is true. *What does not kill you only makes you stronger.*

Everyone wants to go to heaven, but no one wants to die. This is a relevant line when it comes to getting out of a tough situation. Many people wait and wait for someone else to come and rescue them. At any given point, everyone is going through some kind of struggle in their lives. Everyone is either focused on getting out of those situations or is focused on reaching the next stage in their life/career/success. Staying idle is the only sure way to regress or even die. Right now, I believe that you want to get out of a tough situation that you are in. Therefore, the first question you must ask yourself is this.

What are you waiting for?

Are you waiting for someone to know about what happened and come to your rescue? Are you waiting for things to change by themselves and offer the next steps to you on a platter? Are you waiting for God to punish those who wronged you so that you get the pleasure of watching it and feel a sense of closure or justice being served?

You need to realise and accept the fact that nothing changes until you take action. Nothing works till you start working.

Have you answered the questions in the previous paragraph honestly? They were actual questions for you to think, analyse and answer (just to yourself).

Are you willing to take action? If you are not willing or if you feel that you are not ready, do not continue. You are not ready for the next exercise. This does not mean that there is something wrong with you. The first time I had to get out of a tough situation, it took me a while. We all gain our life experience through living our lives and going through different experiences. If this is the first time for you, it is possible that you are in shock and unable to even think straight. It is perfectly normal and alright.

Just remember that the longer you brood, the more chances that you will spiral down.

If you answered the questions and you FEEL you are ready, then let us move forward. I stress 'feel' because your feelings are a good indicator of where you are in your readiness. It is not enough to mentally think that you are ready. It is best if you can feel it inside of you. There are times when you should not go only by your feelings. I will talk about it when I share about daily actions that you need to take.

Getting out of a tough situation depends on changing your perspective about the event and training your mind to see the events as they are. **Just as events**. Unfortunately, we naturally tend to have a negative outlook when things do not work in our favour, and we feel like victims.

People with a victim mentality feel and believe that bad things always happen to them. They feel that they have no control over things that happen in their lives and that life just happens to them. If you want to get out of your situation, it is important to ensure that you do not fall into this trap. I have seen many people who find it hard to come out of this mentality. They live the life of a victim. They are constantly seeking sympathy from others with their default 'Poor me'/'Help me'/ 'Look at me' kind of approach. There is nothing wrong with taking help from others, but in this case, they are not asking for real help to get out of a situation. They need others to hear them out and agree with all their feelings and sympathise with them.

Some people do this naturally because this is their normal way of being. It is easy to hide behind all kinds of stories that they make up, where everyone is out to get them, and they can do no wrong. It is always someone else's fault. It takes a lot of courage to look at things objectively, to look at your thoughts and emotions objectively and that is exactly what I would like you to do. Again, the question is: Are you ready for that? If you are not, like I said earlier, don't force yourself through these processes. These can be effective only when you are ready in all respects. Once you get through with this exercise, we can move to the next step which is the What Next Method.

I have come across bits and pieces of all that I am going to share from different people, but I have never seen them put most logically and methodically like my mentor Blair Singer. This is one of the most important sessions he does for his tribe, of which I am proud to be part.

The 4 Stages of Mind Before Reaching What Next Mindset

When something bad happens to us, we go through different phases of reacting to it and handling ourselves. These phases need not be in the sequence that I list here. You may not go through all of these stages either, but it is important to understand each of these and ask yourself some tough questions to know which stage you are currently in. These stages are a combination of some of the stages from the *Grief Cycle model* developed by *Elizabeth Kubler-Ross* and *The Responsibility Process* by *Christopher Avery*. This is all about helping you take responsibility for your life and your actions. Let us get on with the first stage.

DENIAL

Before you take even the first step towards taking responsibility, you need to get over your grief connected to the event or the situation you are in. Denial is a coping mechanism for a lot of people. This especially happens when the event that transpired is emotionally harsh. Denial can happen in various degrees of severity. Maybe you lost a loved one. I have known people who have lived in denial for a long period of time. They act and talk and refer to the person as if they still exist. They mask their real emotions with happy faces and are too stubborn to even consider any other 'reality'. They create a 'make-believe' world where the person still exists and continue to have imaginary conversations with them.

However, denial can happen in various other situations as well. I have had conversations with women who have suffered from domestic violence and in most cases, they live in denial. They say that their husband is not a bad person, and these things happen only once in a while. Some of them even convince themselves that their husbands become violent because of something *they* have done.

When I lost a year, I was in denial for some time. I was still living with my coursemates in the same block for a month until our break started, and I remember putting up a sheet of paper in front of my desk on which I had written '*You are relegated*'. I found myself believing that somehow, miraculously, things would change and I would wake up one day where everything would be normal and I would still graduate with my coursemates. I had to get the message into my sub-conscious through brute force.

I was in denial when I met with the accident. This was more due to a lack of information and understanding of the gravity of the situation. I was in denial that I had been to the edge and back. I convinced myself that I would be out in four to six weeks maximum because that was the time required to recover in case of normal fractures. What I had was fundamentally a fracture, even though my leg below my knee had opened like a bouquet of flowers. Whenever I asked for confirmation about the discharge date from my surgeon, he used to just smile and say, 'We will see.' It helped me then because I don't know how I would have reacted if I had understood the gravity of the situation.

I was in denial with my 'fiancée' because I told myself that she and even my friend could never do something like that. I was convinced that she had not thought this through, and I was desperately trying to make her 'understand'. The more I tried to convince her of my theory, the more irritated she became, and I could not understand why.

You could also be in denial of the fact that you are in the denial stage. The best person to know and identify this is someone close to you, who can tell you the truth with compassion. Reach out to them and find out. Are you in denial of the whole event or incident? Maybe you accepted a situation in your life, but you are in denial of the seriousness of it, like alcohol addiction, for example. You may have accepted the addiction but still could be just brushing it off as something trivial.

You need to ask yourself if you are in denial about what has happened/is happening in your life, and you need to be honest in your response. If yes, then ask how long you have been in this state.

Do you really think that the problem will vanish if you continue to live in denial? I learned through all my experiences that irrespective of how much ever I wanted to live in denial, nothing was going to change till I accepted the reality.

Subconsciously, by being in the denial stage, you are buying time to get used to what has happened. This is normal and healthy for a short duration because you may not be able to face the facts and all the challenges that you must consider once you accept what has happened.

If you agree with me, then it is time for you to get out of the denial stage. One of the most significant aspects of this stage is that you suppress your real feelings and emotions. You put up a front because you are scared to face facts.

Seek help from a trusted friend/partner/counsellor. Talk about your fears. Express yourself. Let the emotions flow. This itself will start the healing process. If you don't feel like talking, then write it down. This process is explained in detail later. The whole idea is for you to express and dissipate your strong emotions associated with the incident so that you reach a point where you can look at things objectively. Even if you don't reach that stage, once your strong emotions subside, you will be able to move past this stage of denial.

BLAMING OTHERS

This common stage that we all go through is nothing recent. It started right inside the Garden of Eden. According to the Bible, God created Adam and Eve and told them not to eat the Forbidden Fruit. They were living happily till the snake appeared and tempted the woman who in turn 'inspired' the man to get the fruit so that they could eat it. When they ate it, they realised that they were naked (the fruit gave them knowledge) and refused to come out when

God came visiting. God realised what had happened (obviously) and asked the man, 'Why did you eat from the Forbidden Tree?'

The first thing that came from him was, 'The woman made me do it!'

When God asked the same question to the woman, what do you think her answer was? Yes, 'The snake made me do it.'

This stage is better than 'denial' because, at this stage, you are willing to accept that something bad has happened, but still, you are not willing to accept the facts. We blame politicians for unrest in our country, we blame the media for how our kids are behaving, and what have you.

There are three kinds of blame games that we indulge in. First is the most common. We blame others for things that happen to us. We see it daily. In our homes, offices, clubs, and everywhere else. From a woman blaming her husband for her unhappiness, to the husband blaming his wife for showing up late at work (because she delayed breakfast!), children (these days even parents) blaming teachers for poor scores, it has seeped into our daily life. This is a comfortable space to be in, but it still does not help you move out of it and do something to move forward. It only feeds your ego that you are the good person and someone else is bad and if they had not done something, you wouldn't find yourself in this situation.

Sometime ago, there was an advertisement on TV for a detergent where a small girl slips and falls into a muddy puddle and her brother (or was it her friend?) promptly starts beating the puddle for making her dress dirty. It was a cute ad, but the message was terrible. You may call me a spoilsport, but these send subtle messages to children as they grow. They start looking for things to blame as soon as something bad happens. I have seen many parents also placing the blame on someone else or something just to stop their children from crying about a loss.

Now the big question: Why do we do that?

First of all, it is easy. You want to blame someone or something else for the incident so that you don't need to be responsible for what happened. And we also don't need to be vulnerable. We feel more in control since we don't need to take responsibility and accept the fact that we may not have done our due diligence, or we may have, without meaning to, contributed to what has happened.

I blamed the truck driver for the accident, I blamed my girlfriend for the breakup, I blamed my friend whom we had trusted with our money. Blaming others rarely helps in any situation. If you are willing to see truthfully, you are basically saying that you have no power over yourself or your situation.

The second type of blaming is blaming yourself. I have seen a lot of people do this almost at a professional level. It's more of self-pity. The poor-me-I-am-not-good-enough-for-anything-bad-things-always-happen-to-me kind of person. All these conversations happen between your two ears, and you convince yourself that you are the reason for everything that happens to you. This is commonly seen in women who are victims of spousal abuse. They have this sad propensity to blame themselves for all that happens to them.

The third kind is blaming God or a higher power for bad things happening in your life. If something beyond your control goes wrong, then the blame goes to God invariably. I blamed God (along with the truck driver) for the accident for a long period. People believe that God punishes them for something they did wrong. Many parents put these thoughts (which later convert to beliefs) into the minds of children by saying God will punish them if they behave badly or if they did wrong things. This is the reason we have more 'God-fearing' people than 'God-loving' ones.

What are you doing in your situation? How is all this blaming exercise working out for you? All the while I was playing the blame game, I was miserable because I was the victim in these scenarios. I wanted bad things to happen to others, somehow wanted to see them suffer for all the things they had 'done to me'. I wanted God to make things right for me since he was unfair to me as well. Just the way I realised that none of the blame game was helping me, you need to ask yourself if it is helping you get out of your situation in any way at all. If not, why give away all the power to someone else when the only person who can take action is you?

If you find yourself blaming someone else or yourself, just know that this is normal as long as you don't hold on to it for too long, and you don't make it a habit. If you are used to doing it, then it becomes even more difficult when the situation that you are in is grave or the event is traumatic.

Therefore, the question you must ask yourself is this. *'Am I blaming someone, even God, for what has happened to me?'*

Be honest in your introspection. The aim is not to find faults with you or beat yourself up for what happened. The aim is to get out of this pit.

JUSTIFICATION

This is another stage that we all go through. Some people spend their entire lives in this stage. In this stage, we basically create a story or a narrative in which situations and events are beyond our control or convince our perceptions as the absolute truth for basing our actions. It is more powerful than lying because we are convinced that nothing is our fault and that what we did or said was the right thing under the circumstances. This is a chronic stage of self-preservation where we are not even willing to accept another point of view and will argue vehemently with others who may be trying to help us see a different perspective.

There is always a 'valid reason' for why things happened and why things are the way it is. It is just another way to protect themselves from taking responsibility. We all know that smoking is injurious to health but if you ask any smoker, they will justify why they do it, despite knowing the ill effects. The same attitude and mindset bleed into all other aspects of life as well. This is a brilliant cover that protects us from mental and emotional pain that we may have to face if we are willing to face the facts.

If we look at our normal daily lives, we justify all our improper actions. It is a human thing to do. From being late for a meeting to using bad words, shouting, or getting into a fight, to killing someone, there is always a justification, the saddest one being, 'I didn't know'. When I got wiped out financially, the only way I could deal with it was by trying to justify to myself that it was right on my part to totally trust the person with whom we invested. 'I didn't know anything about investing in the stock market', 'I didn't know how to read financial documents about investing', 'How could I check the authenticity of the documents he gave me without proper knowledge?', 'Maloni was a CA. If she could not figure it out, how could I?' and all that.

It helped me sleep at night because I convinced myself that it was all his fault, and I did the right thing by trusting him because Maloni trusted him. I was not ready to go through the regret that I was the one who messed up something that we had worked so hard for. I could not face the fact that I did not even try to validate the stories he told me all through.

I have come across people who have lived in bitterness and anger all their lives because of some incidents where some people have been bad to them. They justify their anger towards the incident(s) that took place, sometimes in their childhood, to hold on to their anger and bitterness. They call it 'righteous anger'. It could be a father holding anger towards his daughter who married against his wishes, could be a sibling who felt that parents were more affectionate or partial to the other one and so many more such examples. It is almost impossible to help them because they hold on to their version of the incident so strongly that they will reject any other suggestion or viewpoint. 'You did not go through what I went through / If you were in my shoes, you would understand' are some of their favourite lines.

This is again about being in a position of having no power over or within themselves. They are angry/frustrated/upset because of something outside of them. Unless those circumstances change, whatever they are holding on to is fully justified.

It is said that we live a 'reason-able' life, but we have changed its connotation to mean that we have a reason for everything that happens in our lives. We live in the story of 'If that didn't happen, I would have been successful, I would have been happy' and all those excuses. Psychologists even have a term for it—*Cognitive Dissonance*.

Irrespective of what it is called by psychologists, I prefer to call it escapism. A wilful act of shirking responsibility. There is an interesting story that I read where some people tracked down the two sons of a drunkard and found one to be a drunkard like his father and the other, a successful businessman and a teetotaller. When asked the reason for how they turned out to be who there were, both said something similar to 'What else did you expect with a father like that?'

Both were subjected to the same situation, but one took it as an excuse and justified his alcoholism by blaming his father while the other took it as a lesson on how not to be and took responsibility for his life and future.

Now the questions you have to ask yourself are: Are you in justification mode? Do you give reasons that are based on other people or incidents for what has happened to you? It doesn't even have to be something big. Look at your normal, everyday life. What is the reason you give to others and yourself when you are late to the office or for a function, when your business is not doing so well, when you are not able to lose weight? Chances are that you would be justifying all these actions and attributing reasons to external things.

We, as humans, are extremely clever at justifying our actions. If you want to know how good you are, just decide that from tomorrow morning, you will get up at 0500 h and go for a run. Set the alarm and sleep. As soon as the alarm rings, you will be amazed at all the convincing reasons you tell yourself as to why you need more rest, that too just for that day and you will start with renewed energy the following day. If you are smiling reading this, I know for a fact that you have experienced this.

Just know that it's quite natural to do it at times but it should not become your default response. The fact is that even when I created justifications, I knew at the back of my mind that this approach was not going to help me move ahead. I knew it every single time.

Justification makes you feel that there is nothing that you can do about the situation. The moment you do that, you are back in victim mode, waiting for the situation to change and you choose to hide behind these 'insurmountable/helpless situations'.

If you are doing any of that, it is time to realize that you are in justification mode and if you are ready to get out of this situation, I will tell you how.

QUITTING

All the stages described above are mindset issues, but this is the worst stage where we feel like there is no hope, there is no point in even trying. The whole world seems dark and gloomy, and we feel that we are all alone in this world and no one and nothing can help us. We are convinced that nothing good can ever happen based on our current situation.

Why do I say this is the worst? Because in all the rest, there is still a will to continue. Even though you are not in the driver's seat, you are willing to at least not give up. However, if you feel ready to quit, it means you must seek professional help at the earliest.

Always remember that any time you feel like quitting, it is just an indication that you are focused on the problem or the challenge and not on the solution or the way out. You feel that your problem is unique to you and there is no solution for it. You feel that if you quit, you might feel better. You are filled with self-criticism, self-hatred, and fear.

If you feel like quitting, just know that the best people have been there. There would be moments in most people's life when they wanted to give up, quit, or even kill themselves. You are no exception. If you listen to their reason, you may feel that yours is worse. It doesn't matter what the situation is. What matters is how you feel and what you feel like doing next. Some people have faced it for a longer time than others, some people go through it multiple times in life. The fact is that we have all been there.

Do you feel that you are at a point of no return? The good news, if you would like to see, is that the only way for you from here is up. All you need to do is seek help and take action.

Maybe you feel like whatever happened to you was beyond your control. You had no say in an accident that happened. Maybe you gave your everything in a relationship and it still did not go as you expected, maybe the illness you are faced with has happened despite your healthy lifestyle. Yes, I understand that at times, things do happen for which you don't find ready answers. The more you insist on finding logical reasons for what happened, the more frustrating it can get.

Always remember that irrespective of what happened you are 100% responsible for how you are planning to move forward in life. In the worst case, where you may not even have the gift of a long life, you still are responsible for how you live every moment of what you have left. I love the quote that goes, *'I cried for the shoes I didn't have until I saw someone who did not have legs.'*

When you are on the verge of quitting, nothing sounds logical to you. You may have someone's number that you have promised to call when you are on the edge, but the darkness around you is so encompassing that you don't even feel like calling that person. The emotional abyss that you have fallen into is so painful that even death starts looking like a better option. Maybe you are frustrated with your job, maybe you can't find any happiness in your marriage, maybe you tried hard but lost, maybe you lost your loved one and nothing and no one can replace them. What you are going through is ripping your heart and mind apart. 'Anything would be better than this,' you may be telling yourself.

If you are there, I need you to stop right now. I just need you to know that what you are feeling is real, but you always have the strength and courage to wait for one more day. Quitting is always an option for you. It is easy. Let us give it one more day and see if anything changes. I truly believe that if you are reading this, you are someone who wants to move forward. You are here looking for solutions or a way to keep going forward. That itself takes you out of the 'Quitter's Mentality' because a quitter will only look for reasons to quit, not to move forward.

Irrespective of which stage you may be in, getting out of any stage has to start with the right mindset. Any amount of skill sets, and techniques will be of no use unless you develop the right mindset. There is only one way you can get out of the situation that you are in—by taking 100% responsibility.

I can literally hear the resistance coming from your mind chatter. *How can I take 100% responsibility when it was not my fault? When it was not in my control?* I agree to everything that you are telling me but answer just one question for yourself. Do you really want to get out of the situation that you are in? Remember, the first step always is your willingness. If someone is drowning, the only way he can be saved is if he *wants* to be saved. I assume that since you are still reading this, you have the willingness.

CHAPTER 15

THE WHAT NEXT METHOD

Congratulations on reaching this chapter! The entire book was about the challenges that I faced, my feelings and how I came out of each situation in order to move forward. You may have gone through similar challenges in your life, maybe more, maybe less. Irrespective of what you may have gone through, if you are struggling to get out of the situation, this chapter might help you do just that.

I do not claim that this method will solve every single challenge of yours. However, if you do this diligently, you will be able to see things in a different light and you will get some direction and inspiration about what you can do so you can move forward. The fact is that life always moves on. It does not wait for you or me. It is up to you and me to keep moving forward. There is no guarantee that there will not be more challenges in your life. But if you do these processes and follow the steps, you will get better at handling your challenges and your turn-around time will keep getting better. Also, once you learn these, you can become a huge help and a blessing to any of your near and dear ones to help them get out of their situations as well.

I hope you have gone through the previous chapter regarding the What Next mindset. If you haven't, you must go through it properly because if you are here without willing to take 100% responsibility of your life and your future, these methods will not help you much and you will not be inspired enough to take action.

Assuming that you are ready to take 100% responsibility, let us dive into the first one.

The first step towards recovery is to be able to dissipate your emotions. When something drastically goes wrong in our lives and we are highly emotional, always remember that the emotions are *a result*. They are the result of some thoughts that are unconstructive, even destructive, rooted in the future and are normally a derivative of some fear that you have. When you go through a breakup, your accompanying thoughts could be that you are not good enough, you will end up living alone, you will never again find happiness or something else along those lines. If you suffer a financial loss, your emotions will likely be based on thoughts that you will die poor, you will never be financially successful, you will not be able to provide for your family, et cetera. If it is the loss of a loved one, it will also have something similar that address the three stages I mentioned earlier.

Whenever something big and bad happens, suddenly, you go into shock because you don't expect something like that to happen. If you are in a serious relationship, you expect it to go well; if you take your pet out, you expect to come back with the pet; when you invest money, you expect it to give at least minimum returns; and when you step out to go to work, you expect to come back home alive. When it doesn't happen, suddenly, you see all the future hopes and dreams associated with that person or thing crumbling down, creating a huge vacuum in that place. Since it is a sudden vacuum, you don't have anything to fill that space and you feel as if you are part of the vacuum.

To that vacuum, your mind and thoughts will start to release powerful negative emotions. These emotions tend to be so powerful that you get sucked into it and are unable to see anything else. You really need to dissipate the emotions so that you can think clearly. Let me remind you of one of the greatest truths I had shared earlier from my mentor, Blair Singer - *"When emotions are high, intelligence is low".* This exercise can help you look at the situation objectively and intelligently.

I need you to write about your incident. I need you to write every single detail, every single thought, evert single emotion associated with the incident. It must be long, and it must be descriptive. If someone 'broke your heart', write down what that person meant to you, what were you expecting from the relationship, how you felt when it ended, what you feel about the other person for doing it, how much you are hurting... Remember, every single detail. You can even write it as a letter addressing the person. You are not to post it or give it to that person because this is an exercise for *you*. Write down all your fears associated with the incident. If you lost a near and dear one, write down all the memories and what that person meant to you, how you saw that person, how you wish you had not lost the person, and what you wish for them wherever they are.

The whole idea is to express it completely. Do not type it on a word document. Write it down on a sheet of paper. You may need many sheets. If you are doing it right, you will break down and you are supposed to. It is not a 'fact-writing' exercise. It is an 'expression of feelings and emotions' exercise. When I wrote one of these letters, I was weeping throughout the exercise. Tears do heal and it is important that you let them out.

The second stage of the exercise is for you to read the letter out loud to someone. It could be your best friend who knows everything about you or an absolute stranger who knows nothing about you. It doesn't matter. If you cannot find anyone, do it in front of a mirror. It is ideal to have someone listen to you. Now the person listening should not do anything except listen with a neutral expression. No words of sympathy, no comforting gestures, no empathising by sharing a similar experience from their life, and no advice.

You will again become emotional while reading the letter aloud. Do not hold back or try to control your emotions. Just be real. Once you finish reading, read it aloud again. Do the same exercise at least a few times. I assure you that by the fourth or fifth time, the strength of your emotions will be much less potent, and you will feel much better. The aim is to repeat this exercise until the emotion is dissipated. You really need this.

At the end of the exercise, when you feel much more in control, you should either tear the sheets off or burn them while telling yourself that you choose to release this incident. This is a powerful exercise, which if did properly, will make you feel light. You will feel like you can move on to the next step.

Now that your strong emotions are released, you should feel much calmer and more grounded. Before we get in to action, we now need to change our vibration. Why is it important? Science has proven that we all are composed of energy fields. Our body is composed of energy producing particles that are in constant motion and like everything else in the universe, we are constantly vibrating, creating, and releasing energy constantly. The Law of Attraction says that we attract other things, people, and events to match our vibrational energy. When you are going through a difficult phase and are emotional, your vibrational energy is low. Once you release the pent-up emotions, your energy has the possibility of coming to a neutral state.

Now we need to change it from neutral to high or positive energy. You don't need to feel bad or guilty about doing that. It does not take away anything from what you have been through. In fact, it is a sign that you are fully prepared to move forward from that incident.

How do you change your vibration? It is much easier than you think. Two energies that have the highest vibrations are *love* and *gratitude*. As human beings, we lose sight of small but important things in our lives quickly. Let us change that. You are going to make four lists right now.

First, I want you to list down 10 things you love about yourself. Not your skills, but your personality traits. You should reflect on who you are and all the good things about you. When you write, don't just write a few words. Be descriptive. If you are a kind-hearted person, don't simply write 'Kindness'. Write something like, 'I am a kind-hearted person. I always try to help people who are in need, and I feel good about the fact that I am kind-hearted.' List out the 10 things about you along these lines.

The second list is where you write 10 things that you love about your friends and family. If a friend cheated you, it doesn't mean that all your friends will. Even if you don't feel like taking help from anyone or even talking to someone, when you do this, you will realize what a great support system you have in your life. It is just that you don't depend on it or use it frequently and in the worst case, you take them for granted. Open your heart and mind and make this list.

The third list you need to make is a list of 10 things that you love about this world. The whole world might look dark and gloomy to you right now, but if you look carefully, you will find so many things that you love about this world that you live in. It could be your community, society, city, country or even the world.

Now we move into the second phase of list making. If you have done the first phase right, you should be feeling much better already. Next, we focus on gratitude. It is true when they say, '*Count your blessings*'. We normally look at things we don't have and ignore or take for granted the things that we already have.

In this last and final list, make a list of 20 things that you are grateful for. Why 20 and not 10 in this? You will understand by the end of this list. We have so many things to be grateful for if we look at things from a place of gratitude. If you are getting three meals a day, you should be thankful because there are so many who don't. If you have a roof over your head, if you are alive, if you can breathe without support, if you can walk without support, if you can see the beauty of this world with your eyes, if you can hear all the beautiful sounds of the world, if you can smell the flowers, a new-born baby, or your favourite aroma, all these counts. Look around, see the world, feel the wind, experience the rain, look at the material things you have, look at the people you have in your life…. If you look for beauty in this world, trust me, you will find it!

Again, you need to write sentences and not just a few words. Be descriptive. Not just 'my eyes'. It should be 'I'm thankful for my eyes because I can see all the beautiful colours in the world, I can see my loved ones.' Once you write down the list, I want you to read it out loud one by one, deliberately feeling the gratitude. By the end of the list, you will be in a totally different vibration.

My daily exercise used to be to write 10 things to be grateful for given that I could not repeat what I had already written the previous day. So, you can imagine how many things I was grateful for by the end of the month. Every month. If you are up to it, you can take this as a challenge. You can rest assured that your life will change in a positive way within a short period of time.

After these two powerful exercises, you should now be able to see things much more objectively. This is where the next step comes, and it is to **separate the facts from the stories** that you have made up in your head, something that I learned first at the *Landmark Forum*. I have heard different versions of this from many amazing trainers and coaches around the world. We are master storytellers, especially when it comes to the tragic kind. We are good at 'catastrophising', which means we imagine the worst case in any situation. Not only that, but we also constantly make up stories of things that happen or don't happen to us on a daily basis.

Let me give you an example. Consider a girl and a boy in love who are highly emotional about each other. One of them calls the other. In this case, let us say the boy calls the girl at about 0800 h and she doesn't pick up the call. He thinks she is busy and after an hour he calls again and still no response. He gets worried and starts calling her again and again at short intervals. There is no response, and he starts panicking. He may get angry/emotional/upset/livid, depending on his nature. He could imagine the following:

1. She wants to break up with me and that's why she is avoiding my calls.
2. She is with someone else (another guy in her office).
3. She has met with an accident… so on and so forth.

Now let us go to the girl's side. She woke up late and was rushing to get ready for work when her boyfriend calls her. After she parks her car, in a hurry to reach the office for a review meeting, she forgets her phone in the car. The review meeting goes on for a few hours.

At lunch, she realised that she doesn't have her phone with her. When she takes the phone from the car, what does she see? 15 missed calls from the boy! Now what do you think is going through her mind?

1. OMG, something has happened to him.
2. He needed me and I was not there.
3. He was in some accident... so on and so forth.

When she calls him back, what kind of mental state do you think she will be in? What kind of mental state do you think the boy will be in after 15 unanswered calls? Do you expect the call to go smoothly? In most cases, no. Why not? Because they both will be reacting to the stories that they have made up in their heads. If they are sensible people, they will calm down in a minute or two, but the start, most likely, will be quite explosive and anxious.

I am not saying that every person is like this. This was just to give you an example of what story-making is and how we do it daily.

The fact is that we learn story-making early in our lives. Children are excellent at making up stories of their imaginary friends, playmates, and about everything in their lives. If you ask them to explain something that happened with them, they can go into explanations that can be irritatingly detailed. This is helpful for them to develop their creative side of the brain. However, we tend to carry that forward into our adult lives and so... story-making comes naturally to us.

We normally make three kinds of stories. First is our story about ourselves. How we see ourselves. You will see some people who are overly confident even if they lack a corresponding level of skills and some who are extremely diffident even though they have excellent skills. Why do you think this happens? It's because of the stories that they make up in their heads.

The second kind are the stories that we make of other people we know and interact with. Have you ever observed that two people can tell you the same thing but it is received differently by you? Parents have this constant complaint. Kids tend to listen and agree with their friends or teachers on the same thing that they disagree with their parents on. This is because of the stories that they have made up about their parents. If you do not like a person at a fundamental level, it is highly unlikely that you will be willing to listen to or accept anything that they say.

The third story that we make up is about the world and life in general. Some people have a positive outlook towards life and get excited about all the technical and digital developments happening in the world. For example, some parents may feel that their children will have great opportunities as they grow up. There could be another person sitting next to him who feels that the world is going to dogs, and our children are going to suffer in the world we are leaving behind for them.

If you have been objective till now, by now, you would understand what I mean by making up stories as well as how and why we make them up. There are always facts associated with an event, which can be proven, which are evidence-based, and then there are stories that we make up which are not proven and don't have any evidence.

Let me give you a simple example. Let us say, you made this statement, 'She broke my heart.'

The question here is, is this a fact or a story that you made because of an event? Factually, if your heart is broken, you cannot be alive. So, it is nothing but a story. The fact is that she chose to end a relationship (for whatever reason). That is all she did. She chose differently. Now depending on what you choose to focus on, your actions will differ. 'She broke my heart' is the victim mentality. 'She chose differently' is objective. Now is the time for you to look back on the event and separate the facts from your stories. It takes a fair amount of objectivity for this to happen. You can take the help of a close friend who is not emotionally invested in the event. Fill up as many statements as you can in the table below. I am giving examples from the events of my life to give you some perspective.

SNo	Event	Story	Fact
1	I was relegated	My coursemates lied to me. They let me down.	All have their versions of the truth. All of them do care a lot for me.
2	The accident changed my future & career	My career & future are finished. I'm finished.	I'm still in the Navy, I must work in a new branch and do well there.
3	My fiancé broke our relationship.	She cheated on me and broke my heart. I hate girls.	She chose someone else. There will be someone else who values me.

The whole aim of this exercise is for you to understand and realise the kind of imaginary things that you have been cooking up inside your head. When you live in your story, you are emotional, you want to get back at people, and you want to see them suffer. When you do that, you are losing all the power that you have within you to change things for yourself.

Once you go through all the stories that you have made up and look at the corresponding facts, you will gain a better grip on the situation. You also will not be emotional (well, not so much) about what has happened after these two exercises.

Now that you have a better understanding of the entire situation, let us move on to the next step. You would have heard this from many people but since you were right in the centre of it, you may not have been able to do it. Here it is.

Identify what is in your control and what is not in your control. There is a powerful quote from Reinhold Niebuhr which goes, *'God, grant me the serenity to accept the things I cannot change, the courage to change the things I can and the wisdom to know the difference.'* For me, the most important part is the last one. Getting the wisdom to know the difference between the two.

If you look around, you will see that most of the anger, sadness, and frustration that people have is because they try to control things that are not in their control, and they do nothing about what they can. You see it every day when people are stuck in traffic, when the weather is bad, when a lockdown happens, and so on.

We even tie our internal happiness to external events or even validation from others. We have no control over what other people think and do or how they feel about us. We can't stop people from saying bad things to or about us. Unfortunately, many of us insist on having the ability to control every aspect of our lives and of people around us but in reality, there will always be things that happen that are unplanned and out of our control. Now if our happiness is tied to the amount of control we have over events and people around us, when these unplanned and unexpected things happen, it really messes with us.

When something terrible happens, we sometimes insist that things ought to get back to how they used to be. When we lose someone, we argue with God to bring them back. These are all part of the grieving process but since you have reached here, I assume that you are ready to move forward.

Why do I insist on this step? It is because when you are focused on things that are not in your control, you are frustrated. You are wasting your energy and you are also stuck in misery because things will not change. I am not asking you to ignore these factors, but you should be aware that being in this position will not help you move forward. It is said that when one door gets shut, another one opens, but if you are only looking at the shut door, you will not even see the new door or even a window that has opened for you in the situation.

Once I went through the stages of denial, blaming, and justifying, I realised that I had to focus on things I could control if I wanted to move forward and be happy. When I lost a year, I wanted so badly for the whole thing to be a bad dream, to turn back the clock and reset the day but at one point, I realised that as long as I was in 'wishful-thinking' mode, I was miserable. I had to look at reality and I had to take stock of what was in my control.

After the accident, I went through a period of questioning/blame game with God and bargaining and what not. There was no respite. The mental and emotional pain coupled with the physical pain was unbearable. In this case, I didn't even know what to look forward to since I did not know when I would get out of the hospital.

When I went through the breakup, I reached a point where I realised that I could not change her mind and make her see what I wanted her to see. I had to accept that it was her choice and decision to move on and I could not do anything about it. I had to look at what I needed to do from there to move forward. Similarly, for all the other incidents as well.

Let us look at some of the things that can be in your control. You can choose to understand what you learned from your experience. You can choose to get up every morning and go for a walk/run, you can choose to decide that these incidents are setbacks, but not the end of your life, you can choose to look at all the things that you are still grateful for in your life. Remember that you always, always have a choice.

Now let us get into specifics. You will write down each incident and then write down what is in your control and what is not in your control. I will give my examples to illustrate.

SNo	Incident	What is not in my control	What is in my control
1	Relegation	I have to repeat a year	Do better in studies
			Use the extra time to learn Guitar
			Make new friends, etc
2	Accident	Hospital Duration	How I approach each day
			Develop more guitar skills
			Read a lot
			Write
		Career change	My attitude to the new branch
			How I can apply myself and grow
			How well I can do in this branch
3	Breakup	The relationship that ended	Be grateful for the good times we had
			Not become bitter towards her
			Not typecast all girls
			Apply learning next time

This is an extremely powerful exercise because here you are truly taking control. You are now in the driver's seat. When you focus on the last column, you will start living powerfully and intentionally.

CHAPTER 16

THE ACTION PLAN

How are you feeling after these two exercises? At this stage, you should be thinking with a lot more clarity, you should be less emotional (therefore more intelligent) and you should be able to look at the event quite objectively. If you are thinking along these lines, then your recovery phase is over. Now it is time to move forward.

From my personal experience, I can say with certainty that it is indeed true that *what doesn't kill you only makes you stronger*. You may not feel it right now (I sincerely hope you do), but you are much stronger, emotionally and mentally right now. You need to first accept it and internalize it because it can fuel you further. There is a small exercise for it.

I want you to take out another sheet of paper and write down all the lessons and learnings that you have had from your experience. Write down, or rather, list down your learnings. Be very matter-of-fact. No emotions. Just the facts. No description here. You can also write how it will help you going forward. If required, seek help from a close friend or a mentor, if you have one, so that they can help you identify your learning as well as how it can help you going forward. There is always a lesson hidden even in the seemingly worst situations.

Now the important thing for you to realise is that your learning could be anything and whatever you get as a learning is absolutely fine. You should be happy and 100% in alignment with your truth (whatever it may be for you). That is all.

Once you finish writing your learning and have understood them, let us look at your next steps. Always remember that when you go through something traumatic, there is a tremendous amount of energy that is created within you. You need to channel all the energy into something constructive. When I lost a year, I directed all my energy into learning to play the guitar. I used to spend hours every day (whatever was possible during my training) learning and playing. I was able to play my first song in just under a month. When I lost all my money, I put all my energy and effort into upskilling myself. Fate could take away all the money, but it could not take away who I was and whatever skills I had. I knew that I needed to acquire new skills to get my life back on track. I started with my coaching certification and NLP Practitioner certification during this time.

Three things happen when you do this. First, your mind gets engaged in something constructive that keeps you moving forward. An idle mind is definitely the devil's workshop, and when coupled with the kind of story-making that we tend to do, it becomes a bottomless pit. So, keep your mind engaged with something useful and constructive. Second, you become really good at it. Due to all the energy that you have inside you, you will be able to really push forward with everything you have.

If you still have any residual anger, resentment, or frustration, direct it all towards this new task and you will surprise yourself with the speed at which you become good at it. Third, when you become good at the task, your self-esteem starts rising. It is easy for me or other people to tell you that external events should not decide how you see yourself. This is true but when you actually go through something tragic, you become doubtful of yourself, and your confidence takes a big hit. You really need a win at this point. To feel good about yourself, to feel that you are not as useless as you thought you were, to feel that you can get your life back.

You need to decide what you are going to focus on and divert your energy to. I will take you through practical steps for you to do just that.

Hopefully, you have decided on what you want to do/to achieve in the next six months (for example). It could be in the next one year as well. If it is longer, you need to break it down into smaller chunks so that you can measure your progress. Why do you need to measure it? Because you can control and adjust what you measure. Maybe you have a goal to make money and be rich. That is not going to happen overnight or in a few months. You need to have a proper plan, where you have milestones to achieve every month or every few months.

Now, let us come to your goals. I don't want this to be like any other goal setting. Many people set their goals, but they fail to achieve them due to various reasons. One main reason is that most of the time, the goals are purely left-brain oriented. They are just numbers and things to achieve. There is no emotional investment into the goal. We know that emotions are powerful and if channelled the right way, they can help you achieve mighty things. That is exactly what we will do right at the start of this exercise. This is not just about achieving a goal; this is about your life and how you can use the lowest point in your life to fuel your growth and transform your life. Trust me, it is possible. I will take you through the steps, but you need to give it your 100%.

Step 1 → Write down that ONE goal that you want to achieve

This goal should be something that inspires you to take action. Ideally, it could be scary for you when you think about it. Could be something that you may have put on the back seat for a long time. It could be something that you *have* to do in order to grow or even to survive. (For example, you may have lost the breadwinner in your family, and you have never worked before but now you have to, and it scares you).

I'm here to tell you that you can do it. I will take you through all the steps that you need to achieve what you want. *The journey of a thousand miles begins with a single step* and this is that step. Write it down, whatever it maybe.

It is also possible that you may be confused about what goal to set especially if you are currently clueless about how to move forward. If that is the case, look at your life right now and see what would make the biggest impact in your life. Else, think of what will make you happy in life. Pick one for now, for the sake of going through the steps. Once you get a grip of the steps to be followed, you can apply the same steps to any number of goals that you want to achieve. Consider this as your template.

Let me give you examples:

- I want to get qualified for a job.
- I want to make money.
- I want to get fit.

The second part to this exercise is make your goals specific. This is important because, the clearer you are about what you want to achieve, the quicker your mind will start working, much more efficiently, towards achieving it.

Let me continue with the same examples.

- I want to become a CA/CS/MBA/Life Coach/Fitness trainer/Yoga instructor, etc.
- I want to earn 1L/2L/3L every month
- I want to be 75Kgs and run a marathon.

Whatever mind chatter is rising to stop you, just brush it aside and go ahead. Write down your audacious, ambitious goal. Your life is about to change. Be excited about it. Remember that one small action is more valuable than listening to a thousand hours of inspirational talks, and you are doing exactly that.

STEP2 → WRITE DOWN HOW ACHIEVING THIS GOAL WILL POSITIVELY CHANGE YOUR LIFE

This is another important step. The first five steps are crucial because they deal with the internal stuff. You know I always talk about mindset v/s skillset and how having the right mindset can help you achieve any skillset. Here also, before you get on with your actions, you should know deep inside how achieving the goal that you have set will impact your life and maybe the life of your loved ones. These aspects will continue to motivate you if or when the going gets tough along your journey.

- When I become a CA, I will be independent, and I will be able to start my own practice/get a job where I will be able to provide for my children/parents/myself.
- When I make 2L per month, I will be able to lead a good and comfortable life/will be able to provide my family with the best of things.
- When I lose weight and get fit for a marathon, I will look and feel good, I will eat healthy, I will have to lose my bad habits to achieve this, and I will live a long and healthy life.

I have consciously used 'when' instead of 'if' because when you write 'if', there is still some doubt whereas, 'when' is definite. It is just a matter of time. The aim here is to attach your goal to have the impact it will have on your life. How your life can totally turn around and what it will look like when it does. This will give momentum to your motivation and determination to work towards your goal.

STEP 3 → WHAT WILL HAPPEN WHEN YOU ACHIEVE YOUR GOAL

This has three sub-sections to it. Imagine that you have achieved your goal in the specified time duration. Now you need to write down the following:

- → How will you feel after achieving your goal?
- → What will you see when you achieve your goal?
- → What will you hear when you achieve your goal?

Now, this is a major step in this process. Here you are internalising everything that will happen when you achieve your goal. You must make these as real as possible for you. Here, you attach your emotions to your goals. Most people don't get into such detail when it comes to setting goals. They just go about 'doing' it. This step will make your goals feel more real than ever before. Let me explain the step further for you.

How will you feel after achieving your goal?

Let us continue with the same examples.

- When I become a CA, I will feel great and confident about myself because now I can earn money for my services. No one can take that away from me.

- When I start earning 2 Lakhs a month, I will feel great and confident because I don't have to depend on anyone else to look after my family. I can take care of my children/parents/siblings and more than anything else, I can work towards becoming rich by learning and investing my money.
- When I lose the extra weight and run a marathon, it will give me confidence like never before. I will feel awesome to wear the clothes that I always wanted to wear, be an example to other people who may be struggling with their weight and fitness. People will take advice from me and will want to follow my example.

WHAT WILL YOU SEE WHEN YOU ACHIEVE YOUR GOAL?

- When I become a CA, I will see admiration in my children for taking charge of my life and theirs too. I would see the appreciation of my parents, friends, and colleague for achieving this despite my difficult circumstances. I would see myself as a winner and an achiever.
- When I start earning 2L a month, I will see the admiration from my family and my friends. I will see them celebrating my achievement and encouraging me to move ahead. I will see money in my bank account every month that can take care of all my needs as well as that of my loved ones.
- When I lose weight and get fit, I will see a younger-looking and fitter me every day in the mirror. I will see other people looking at me and admiring my transformation. I will see many of my friends calling me for advice, asking me to help them achieve the same. I will see myself as an example of how dedication and discipline can bring about massive transformations.

What will you hear when you achieve your goal?

- When I become a CA, I will hear others talking about what a determined person I am. I will hear my family talking how proud they are of me and my achievement.
- When I start earning 2L a month, I will hear happy conversations from my family. I will hear them talk about how responsible I am towards them. I will hear friends telling my name as an example of how to bounce back from difficult situations.
- When I lose weight and get fit, I will hear my friends and co-workers telling me about my dedication and determination towards my health. I will hear them quote me as an example to inspire others. I will hear people saying if you can do it, I believe I can as well.

These three things will give you the inspiration to work towards your goal. When it gets difficult for you along the way, these will keep you moving forward. You will know your situation, your family, co-workers, friends well. You will know what they will say about you, what you will feel, see, and hear when you achieve your goal. Make it as descriptive as possible so that you have a clear picture that you can carry in your mind and heart.

Step 4 → Explore your roadblocks or fears that can stop you from achieving your goal

This is another important step in your journey towards achieving your goals. A true leader will anticipate difficulties or roadblocks and fears that might come up and be prepared to meet them. These should not come up along the way and surprise you. And if they do, you should be prepared to handle them. If you do not prepare ahead for them, you might sabotage your success because of these fears.

Roadblocks and fears can be of four types.

1. **Emotional Roadblocks** → These are mostly fears that are based on your emotions. You may feel that you may lose something that is emotionally close to you when/if you go about achieving your goal that you have set for yourself.
   - If I want to become a CA, I may need to put in long hours of study and I will lose the time that I have currently with my family.
   - If I want to earn 2L a month, I may have to do things that I have never done before and I fear doing things that I am not used to doing.
   - If I want to lose weight, I may have to join a health club and go in the mornings, and I will not be able to spend the time with my kids. I will have to stop making the tasty food that I make as I will have to shift to a healthier diet. I won't be able to make and eat the things my parents lovingly make for me every day.

2. **Mental Roadblock** → These are fears based on the logic that you have made up for yourself. We all have certain realities that we have defined for us, and we live within the limitations of these beliefs.
   - To be a CA, I must be good with numbers, but I am bad at numbers. The CAs that I know were good with numbers right from their younger days. I will have to attend many classes and I do not have the time for them and do the homework that come with those classes.

- To earn 2L a month, I must be really good at something and right now, I have no special skills. It will take me too much time and effort to reach a position where I earn 2L per month.
- To lose weight, I may have to join a gym or go for runs every day and I have never been to a gym. Due to my current weight, it may not be possible for me to start running. My knees will get damaged. I am not good at cooking. My cook prepares normal dishes which may not be the healthiest option for me to lose weight and get fit.

3. **Physical Roadblocks** → These are again fears that we make up looking at circumstances like time, distance, effort, etc.
   - To be a CA, I need to find a good institute and I don't have any good institutes near where I stay. I am not good with online learning and these days most classes are online. I don't have a good laptop to do online learning.
   - To earn 2L per month, I need to start working somewhere and I do not even have a resume to start with. I don't know who will hire me for the skillsets I have. To start my own business, I need to register a business and then take care of all the logistics, accounting, etc.
   - To lose weight and to get fit, I need to reach the health club which is far, and I don't know how to drive there every day. I live in a place that does not have much space for running as it is in the middle of a busy street. There are no parks nearby where I can walk every day.

4. **Spiritual Roadblocks** → These are interesting as they stem from your deep-rooted beliefs about money, work, family, values, etc. You will really need to go deep to find out if you have any blocks based on these aspects. I'm just giving you a few examples here. Some of these could be at a subconscious level.

- If God wanted me to be a CA, then He would have made me really good with numbers.
- If I run after money, bad things will happen because I believe that money is the root of all evil.
- If I lose weight and get fit, I might lose my identity in my family as all my family members are on the heavier side and they are happy with themselves even though it is not healthy. I don't want to be the black sheep of my family. This particular one may seem far-fetched, but I have coached people who were not able to lose weight despite exercise and diet. When I took them through a process it was revealed that this was their subconscious block that stopped them from losing weight (much to their shock).

Now, it is not necessary that you have all the four roadblocks. You may have only one from all these or you may have many under one type of roadblock itself or you may have something from each type. It doesn't matter even if you have one from each category. Know that whatever fears or roadblocks you have are normal. We are all human and we have our fears. Just ensure that you list down everything.

Now I will take you through the steps to overcome all this and move towards achieving your goal.

STEP 5 → EXPLORE INTERNAL RESOURCES

To overcome any roadblocks or fear that stops you, we need resources. Unfortunately, most of the time we are focused on external resources to solve our challenges and handle our fears. We have a huge reservoir of internal resources at our disposal which we rarely tap into. You see these resources in action when you are in a life-threatening situation. There may have been situations or incidents in your life where you did something, took action, made some spot decisions, and later, when you looked back, wondered how you were able to do all that. Those are the times when you tapped into your internal resources. These are more powerful than any external resources that you have around you. Most of us are not even aware of the strengths that we have inside of us.

To help you understand, I will give you a list of values, strengths that people have. See what resonates with you. Don't try to study each of these qualities and try to analyse and see if you have it. Just look at the list below and write down three to five qualities that jump out of this list.

Adaptable	*Confident*	*Friendly*	*Love*	*Reasonable*
Acceptance	*Constructive*	*Generous*	*Loyal*	*Relationships*
Action	*Cooperative*	*Gentle*	*Motivated*	*Reliable*
Agile	*Courage*	*Gratitude*	*Networking*	*Resilience*
Ambitious	*Courteous*	*Healthy*	*Observant*	*Risk Taker*
Artistic	*Creative*	*Honest*	*Optimistic*	*Self-Direction*
Assertive	*Decision*	*Humble*	*Organised*	*Self-Starter*
Authentic	*Dedicated*	*Influencing*	*Passionate*	*Stable*
Balanced	*Dependable*	*Inspired*	*People Person*	*Tireless*
Brave	*Detachment*	*Integrity*	*Persistent*	*Trustworthy*
Calm	*Determined*	*Intelligent*	*Playful*	*Unassuming*
Caring	*Devotion*	*Kind*	*Positive*	*Unbiased*
Challenging	*Diligence*	*Knowledgeable*	*Practical*	*Understanding*
Cheerful	*Energetic*	*Leadership*	*Presence*	*Vigilant*
Committed	*Enthusiastic*	*Listening*	*Principled*	*Vocal*
Communication	*Faithful*	*Lively*	*Rational*	*Warm*
Competitive	*Flexible*	*Logical*	*Realistic*	*Wisdom*

These are your internal strengths that will help you achieve your goal. Just keep it limited to three or max five. It could also be something that is not in this list. You know yourself the best. Think of who you are and how you have displayed some strengths in times of crisis before.

Maybe you are diligent in what you do. Maybe you are someone who loves to take up challenges. It could be anything. Once you write them down, think of ways you can use these internal strengths to achieve the goal that you have set for yourself.

STEP 6 → EXPLORE EXTERNAL RESOURCES

What are external resources? External resources can be anything that you can take help from. Think and make a list of everyone in your family, friends, co-workers, and professionals who can help you achieve your goal. Think of courses that you can/must do. Think of people who can help you in other ways. Maybe you have kids, and you need some help from friends and family to look after them while you are busy with classes or courses.

List down the skills that you may need to acquire to achieve your goal. Find out how you can achieve those skills. Find out about the finances required and how to drum up those finances. You need to be shameless here. Remember that you are working towards building your life. It matters to you and your family the most. Nothing else really matters. Also, your friends and family will be more than willing to help you out if you ask them. Make your list and do not hesitate to ask people for help.

STEP 7 → WHAT YOU HAVE TO DO

Now comes the action plan. Remember, *'To get what you never had; you must start doing things that you have never done.'* You know your internal strengths; you have your external resources listed out. Now what are the things you need to DO to achieve your goal?

Write down at least three habits, skills, and behaviours that you need to adopt to achieve your goal. You may have to start waking up an hour early every day from now. You may have to seek and find a mentor from whom you can take guidance regularly. You may need to change all the food and ingredients at home to healthy foods. You may have to take help from your spouse who can contribute by earning some additional income that adds to the goal you have for your family. List all the things that you must do to achieve your goal.

STEP 8 → WHO YOU HAVE TO BE

This becomes the crux of your journey forward. Something that my mentor, Blair Singer, always stresses upon. He always says that *whatever you achieve in your life is always a function of who you are and who you are willing to be as a person.* Your success, your achievements are all tied to who you are willing to be.

The sequence is always BE→DO→HAVE.

To HAVE what you want to have, you must DO what is necessary and to do it effectively, you have to BE that person who have the will, determination and the right mindset. It is always about 'being' more than 'doing'.

Look at yourself and ask. Who do you have to BE to achieve your goal? Do you have to be more disciplined? Determined? Driven? Committed? You may show anything to the outside world, but you can never lie to the person in the mirror. This is where you come clean about yourself. You know your bad habits, your bad attitude, your unconstructive behaviours that can sabotage the achievement of your goal. List them down and look at them. Ask yourself, WHO DO YOU HAVE TO BE if you need to kick these away from your life?

STEP 9 → EXPERIENCE THE OUTCOME

This is the one before the final step in your goal-setting process. By the time you reach this step, you will feel more relaxed, confident, and even inspired towards achieving your goal because you are no longer aimless. You know what you want, and you have identified all the resources to achieve your goal. You don't feel desperate and clueless anymore.

Achieving any goal is not just about 'doing' and 'being', it is also connected with your energies. It is important that you are in the right frame of mind so that you attract the success towards you. This is where this step comes in. This is a step that I strongly recommend that you do every morning as you wake up and do it again just before you go to sleep.

The Law of Attraction says that you always attract things to you based on the energies and vibrations that you send out to the universe. We are sending out vibrations constantly when we are upset, when we are angry, when we are happy and when we are grateful. We are constantly asking the universe through our vibrations, and it always brings more of what we ask for, both positive and negative.

The way to do the exercise is to sit down comfortably on a chair and close your eyes and visualise you achieving your goal. Make it as vivid as possible. What you look like, what you are wearing, people around you, what you are seeing, feeling, and hearing from others, every small detail should be included. The more vivid it is, the more powerful it becomes, the greater the chances of manifestation of that goal.

I am not saying this to give you a good feeling. Top athletes and performers do this visualisation exercise regularly. The subconscious mind does not differentiate between you actually doing it and visualising it. I have visualised about publishing my book several times and that is the reason I have reached till this point. Will things happen automatically just because you visualise it? It won't, but it will bring in people into your life who will help you/drive you/nag you into accomplishing your dream. Do this at least for 5 to 7 minutes at a time. Hold that visual in your mind and make it real. You must feel the vibrations all over your body. That is when you know your visualisation is powerful.

STEP 10 → ACTION TIME

Well, nothing works until you start working. Until now, it was only planning. Now, it's action time. I need you to list down minimum three things you will do in the next seven days that will take you towards your goal. It can be something small, but it needs to be done in the specified time.

Be sure to list date of completion for these actions.

You also need to find an accountability partner. Someone to whom you will be accountable for taking these actions within the time or date given. We are our biggest enemies. As time goes by, the pain that drove you into action will ease and the determination that you had at the start may begin to wane. That is where your accountability partner comes in. This person will keep you on track by reminding you, inspiring you or even insulting you (not what I recommend, but depends on you). Whatever works best for you. It is important to find the right person who knows you well enough to handle you. I normally advice against spouses from being accountability partners because many times, things can… go bad.

For me, it has always been my best friend. It is totally your choice but make sure that you choose the right person.

Well, there you have all the steps covered to make your goals and dreams come true. It is not going to be easy, but I have given you a structure and guidance on how you can achieve what you want to achieve.

WHAT NEXT...AFTER WHAT NEXT!

Being alive is like being on a horse. It keeps moving. Days and nights pass, and nothing waits or stops for anyone. We do go through good days, bad days, and horrible days. It is up to each one of us to handle these and keep moving forward. We all have responsibilities and commitments, first to ourselves and to our loved ones. It is easy to hide behind a traumatic event and let our lives get wasted. We can hide behind alcohol and other substances and live in the stories that we have made up for ourselves. In all likelihood, you would know at least a few people even in your circle who do that. Some do it to a small degree whereas some others choose to dedicate their entire lives to live in the cycle of denial-blaming-justifying. They refuse to move on or even look ahead.

I believe you picked this book because you are not one of them. Even if you were one of them, I do really hope that you are now in a position to move forward. With all its sham and let-downs and heart breaks, life is still beautiful, and you can make it even more beautiful. It is all in your hands and only in your hands. I wish you the best that life has to offer, and I know that you truly deserve it. Its time you believe it as well.

EPILOGUE

Finally, it started raining. Hopefully, monsoons reached Hyderabad, a place that I have grown to love. Watching the rain is beautiful in the county that we live in. I can soak in the smell of fresh earth here. The bliss was real as I sat stretched on my recliner in our living room. When I looked up to share a silly joke someone had forwarded, my heart simply melted. I could see Pallavi sitting to my left on the sofa, working on a script for an event. She has this way of staring intently at the screen when she is utterly focused. If concentration had a face, this would be it. Right across me sat Giaa, practising her guitar. Sometimes I cannot believe the miracle we created. Somehow, she has managed to take the best qualities from us and build on it, making them better. She is just fourteen and she plays the guitar beautifully. You know, she can play *Sweet child of Mine* by Guns 'n' Roses like a boss. I never got a chance to learn guitar professionally from an instructor and I wanted her to learn an instrument. I'm so happy that she has become really good with the guitar. Knowing an instrument is like having a constant companion. You are never alone even if you are physically alone.

I got a start as Loki and Milo ran right across my face, chasing each other. There was no respite from them, but who needs a respite from fun and cuteness? These fur balls have changed our lives since they arrived more than two years back. I grew up with my pet dog Kittoo, who was my constant companion during my school days. He was a cross between an Indie and Dachshund making him the size of a normal Indie breed but looked exactly like a Dachshund. There was a time during my school years, when we moved to a rented home since we wanted more rooms than the 2BHK that we were living in. This new home had a huge yard in front which opened into a lovely coconut grove. It was massive and beautiful, but the only issue for me was that there was no other child in the entire colony of about 7 homes. Therefore, every single day after I reached back from school, I used to play with Kittoo for an hour or two till Amma came out and send both of us inside, me to the bathroom and Kittoo under one of the beds to hide.

A pet changes not just you but the whole family. Now that we were living in apartments, I was sceptical about having a dog because we did not have the bandwidth to take it down for walks. Giaa has been asking either for a sibling or a pet for many years and once the lockdown happened, she became even more insistent as she was all alone, and she got tired of having just us around. A pet was naturally the easier choice for us. I was not really a cat person but since a cat was more manageable, we decided to get a kitten for Giaa. Luckily, Uma also got herself a kitten and the same week, we got Loki.

Pallavi was palpitating till Loki entered home because she never had a pet and had no clue if she would be able to handle him. When Loki entered Pallavi had one look at him and she melted (remains so). After a few months, we saw that Loki was bored for the most part of the day as there was a limit to the amount of stuff we could do with him. Therefore, we decided to get him a companion. That's how Milo came into our lives. Now they both do what cats do with each other – play, fight, chase and snuggle and we get to watch them do all the goofy things. Interestingly, our cats also went on us. Loki is like me. Very loving and caring but not expressive at all (except when Giaa is unwell and then he doesn't leave her side till she is fine). Milo is like Pallavi. Very active, very playful, and very expressive.

I smiled as I thought about the space I was in. It was quite blissful for me. I am closer to reaching 50 years of age. We were happy as a family. We were complete as a family. Giaa has grown and continues to grow into a beautiful girl, both inside and out. She is confident, expressive, and compassionate and has an amazing thought process that she shares during our interactions. It's a privilege to see her grow and flourish like this and we both are so proud of her. I am content and happy with my life. Are we back to being millionaires? Not yet. Have we stopped trying? Never! Are we sad about it? Absolutely not! What is the point of trying to make more money if we are not happy and grateful for what we already have?

Gratefulness! A term that many of us use casually. True gratefulness is what opens doors for all beautiful things in life. I have so much to be grateful for. It doesn't require too much imagination to know that a head-on collision between a truck and a bike can end up being really bad for the biker. I received my education in gratitude while I was at the hospital. I was shifted to an Orthopaedic speciality military hospital in Pune for the last 6 months of my hospitalization. My leg had healed quite a bit and I was able to walk with the support of a walking stick. However, my leg was totally disfigured and had healed slightly at an angle, and I was quite unhappy about it. The surgeon there sent me to get braces made for my leg at a place called Artificial Limb Centre in Pune. I spent half a day there and it totally changed my life. There was not a single patient at ALC who had all their limbs. While I was waiting, I saw one man, evidently well built, (must've been close to 6 feet in height) walking around and meeting people with a big smile and I could see that he was genuinely happy. The man was only till his knees. He had two short wooden stumps below his knee on which he walked. It was like a slap on my face. I was cribbing about the scars on my intact leg, and I was seeing happiness in someone who had lost both his legs. I left the place with tears of gratitude and joy for making me understand what gratitude meant.

Think of all the beautiful people and things in your life. It is said that if you have food in your fridge, clothes on your back, a roof over your head and a place to sleep, you are richer than 75 percent of the world. Unfortunately, many of us tend to focus only on the things we don't have.

Today I have so much to be grateful for. An amazing family, my parents, in laws, my sisters, my loving friends, great health, resources to live, cars to drive, pets to love and a safe place to live and so much more. I have Raju back in my active life. Today I work with him. Even though he does not have the time that he used to have earlier for me, I know for a fact that his heart and love for me are still the same. I choose to focus on all this every single day. Have all challenges stopped happening in my life? Not at all. It is a daily affair. It doesn't have to be massive or earth-shattering. It could be something as simple as my alarm not going off, my child having a project submission the next day and she totally forgetting about it. Could be anything. How do I handle these things? How can you handle these things? Just ask yourself the simple question, 'What Next?'

I may have explained 'What Next' as a process. I may have given you step by step method of how you can get out of your pit and the tough situations you are in. However, What Next is not just a process, it is, and it must become a 'way of life'. Remember that your brain and your subconscious mind have all the answers. All you must do is engage them with the right questions, and you will keep getting the right solutions.

When your alarm doesn't ring, instead of asking 'Why me?' or 'Why today?', ask 'What next?' You would know what to do.

When you rush to your car and see a flat tyre, instead of cursing the day and the tyre, just ask 'What Next?'

From the smallest to the biggest challenge that you face daily, make What Next your default mantra and you will never be stuck in life or get sucked into the middle of the problem with no apparent solution.

Even if you come across a massive challenge in your life, remember that this one question with just two words can help you get through any challenge that you face.

Yes, you will go through a period of mourning, especially in the beginning, when you have not practised asking this question. During this time, talk to people, share your feelings and emotions, go through the method shared in the previous chapters and come out of it.

Once you have done that, take a deep breath, smile, and get ready for your life ahead, the next adventure and ask yourself this question. **WHAT NEXT?**

Made in the USA
Monee, IL
03 May 2026